HISTORY of the SCOTS

Book I

Ian Ferguson

Oliver & Boyd

Oliver & Boyd
Longman House, Burnt Mill
Harlow, Essex CM20 2JE
An Imprint of the Longman Group UK Ltd

ISBN 005 003992 X

First published 1987
Second impression 1994

Set in 11/13 Bembo

Printed in Hong Kong
NPC/02

Acknowledgements

The author and publishers are grateful to those listed below for permission to reproduce the following: Antikvarisk-topografiska arkivet, Stockholm, photograph: 45 (top right); Archives de France, photograph: 76 (left); City of Birmingham Museums and Art Gallery, photograph: 50; Trustees of the British Museum, photograph: 56; Controller of Her Majesty's Stationery Office (crown copyright), photograph: 75; Dean and Chapter of Westminster Abbey, photograph: 67; Richard Dennis, photograph: 70; Duke of Roxburghe, photograph: 64; Environment Canada—Parks, photograph: 52 (bottom); Historic Buildings & Monuments, Scotland, photographs: 17 (top), 26, 27, 38 (2), 53; Scottish National Portrait Gallery, photograph: 4 & 5; National Museum of Copenhagen, photographs: 28, 45 (bottom left), 51 (bottom); National Museum of Iceland, photograph: 52 (top); National Museum of Ireland, photograph: 45 (bottom right); National Museums of Scotland, photographs: 8, 17 (bottom), 34, 35, 51 (top), 54 (top), 76 (right); Trustees of the National Library of Scotland, photograph: 9; National Trust for Scotland, photograph: 72; Ronald Sheridan's Photo-Library, photographs: 29 (2), 60; Royal Commission on the Ancient & Historical Monuments of Scotland, photograph: 16 (bottom); Society of Antiquaries of Scotland, artwork: 12, 13, 18 (right); Svenska Turistforeningen's Bibliotek/Bildarkiv, Stockholm, photograph: 45 (top left); University Museum of National Antiquities, Oslo, Norway photograph: 48; Dr Trevor Watkins, photograph: 16 (top)

Illustrations and maps by Donald Harley, Michael Strand and Jeremy Gower

Contents

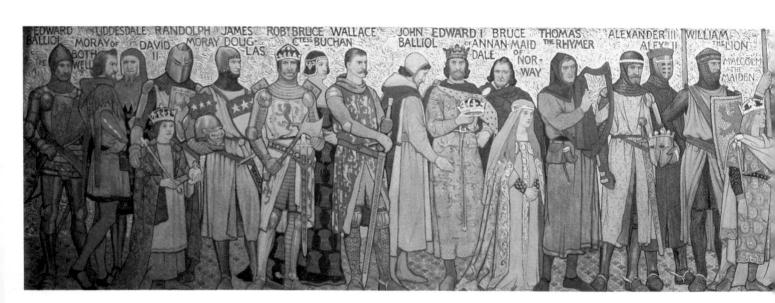

To Caroline

Teachers' Notes

One of the distinctive features of this series is the extensive use of visual and written source material. Although teaching by means of such sources is not new, one of the most interesting and exciting developments is their growing use in the everyday teaching of history. If the purpose of history is to help people in the present to understand those in the past then sources provide an excellent means of allowing us to listen to the authentic voice of the past.

History can also offer another benefit. Through the study of history young people can cultivate an attitude of critical enquiry which will stand them in good stead throughout their lives. Looking at the achievements, failures and follies of the past can provide excellent experience and a perspective on the present. This is one of the reasons for the inclusion of Case Histories. They are there to widen and deepen young people's knowledge of the past. The Case Histories are not intended to be 'debunking' exercises. The whole intention behind them is to show that the great and the famous—and even the Scots!—are only human like the rest of us. Above all, the Case Histories can show that there is more than one version of any event.

Through the narrative and the evidence that is presented in these pages, students will learn to recognise the value of historical evidence and to draw conclusions from it. They will also develop understanding of similarity and difference, continuity and change over time—vital concepts for making sense of today's changing world.

I wish to thank all those teachers and pupils who have helped me by their advice, discussions and arguments in writing this history of the Scots. Any mistakes or infelicities are mine.

Ian Ferguson

John's Complaint

When John visited his grandmother he was full of complaints. 'The whole school had to sit and listen to a boring service in memory of those who were killed in both World Wars,' he said. 'What's the use of listening to all that talk about war, anyway? I don't know anybody who fought in the First World War, far less anyone who died in it.'

His grandmother thought for a moment and said, 'I do. My father, your great-grandfather, was in France all through the 1914–18 War. I've got a picture of him in uniform somewhere.'

She found an old photograph album and showed John a faded picture of a young man dressed in a drab khaki uniform. Though he did not know it at the time, this photograph started John on the search for his own family history.

A Scottish soldier wearing a sheepskin to protect himself from the cold.

John's Search

John's grandmother told him that her father had not spoken much about what had happened to him during the war. 'It's as though he wanted to forget about it,' she said. He had mentioned some things though. He had been wounded and had spent some time in a hospital in England. Her father had called it a 'Blighty wound' because 'Blighty' was the soldiers' name for home. She remembered more things about her soldier-father. She was sure he had begun the war as Private and had been promoted to a Sergeant. She told John there was a trunk in the attic which contained 'old papers and other things' about her father.

In a corner of the attic John found an old, dusty trunk and in it was a treasure-trove of papers, documents and other souvenirs of his great-grandfather's war service. He found a Pay Book which showed how much the young soldier had been paid. It also told him that his great-grandfather had enlisted in the Gordon Highlanders in September, 1914 and had stayed in that regiment until he left the army in March, 1919.

There were also a few faded newspaper cuttings which John's grandmother thought had been cut out by her mother. One of them was a list of soldiers 'Missing in Action, Believed Dead' which had his great-grandfather's name on it. However, another cutting a few days later showed him as 'Wounded in Action'. John had now found out when his great-grandfather had received his 'Blighty Wound'. John thought how sad this soldier's wife must have felt during those days when she thought her husband had been killed.

Another piece of paper, fraying round the edges, was a 'Despatch' from the War Office mentioning the bravery in action of Corporal John Stewart on July 3rd 1916. There were even medals with ribbons attached to them. One of the medals had the inscription on it, 'The Great War for Civilization'. At the bottom of the trunk was a bayonet and John wondered how many times it had been used in battle.

But the best discovery of all was a diary which the soldier had kept for a few months. In it were a soldier's thoughts of what it was like to be in the midst of so much death and suffering.

John took some of his treasures and showed them to Mr Mackie, his History teacher. Mr Mackie told John's class about them and explained that if John's great-grandfather had been caught keeping the diary he would have been severely punished, for if he had been captured by the Germans it might have given them valuable information. Mr Mackie said that the school had its own reminders of the two World Wars for there was a Roll of Honour containing the names of all those former pupils who had been killed in both these wars. Perhaps your school has a Roll of Honour.

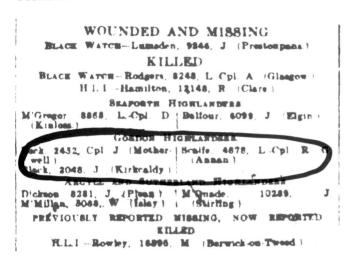

Writing about War

During the next History lesson Mr Mackie showed the class pictures from books about the First World War. He also read them a poem called 'Futility' by a British soldier named Wilfred Owen who had been killed shortly before the war ended in November, 1918. The whole class was quiet as Mr Mackie read these lines about a dead soldier:

> Move him into the sun—
> Gently its touch awoke him once,
> At home, whispering of fields unsown.
> Always it woke him, even in France,
> Until this morning and this snow.
> If anything might rouse him now
> The kind old sun will know. . . .

Mr Mackie lent John one of his own books about the war. The author had written:

Life in the Trenches
Trench wafare was to last on the western front for the next three years. The trenches were deep enough for the men to move around in them without being seen by the enemy. They were defended by strongly-built machine gun posts that looked out over 'no-man's land'. Whenever enemy troops wanted to attack they first had to cross no-man's land.

(H. Gough, *Europe 1763–1970*, Longman, 1974)

Sources of Evidence

As he was looking at all these things about his great-grandfather's life John thought they were like pieces of a jigsaw. As each new piece of evidence was found and fitted into place so a picture began to take shape of one soldier's life during one of the most terrible wars in history. John realised that if he could piece the evidence together he could write part of his own family's history.

He was right when he thought he was collecting the evidence for his own history. What John was doing is exactly the same as a historian does when he is writing a history book. Before he can begin he collects as many sources or different kinds of evidence as he can.

Let's look at the different kinds of **evidence** that John discovered about the history of his great-grandfather. John's grandmother told him about her father and so she gave John **oral** evidence, that is **spoken** evidence. The Pay Book and the newspaper cuttings were different sources for they were **written** or **literary** evidence. The medals and bayonet were another source of evidence. They were made by people during or immediately after the war. They are **man-made** evidence or **artefacts**. An archaeologist who discovers a flint knife from an old grave would call it an artefact. Think what you might call the evidence from a photograph.

While Mr Mackie was showing the class the evidence that John had discovered in the trunk, they noticed that he was sorting it into a different group from the pile of books he had used to tell them about the war. Soon he had a collection at each end of his desk. He asked the class to point to which pile had been made or written during or shortly after the war. The class pointed to the group which contained the diary and the bayonet. Mr Mackie then called these **primary sources** because they were made or written at the time, sometimes by people who had actually taken part in the war. The other pile, the books, he called **secondary sources** because they had been written by historians after the war. When a historian has found as many **primary** sources as he can he uses them to write a **secondary source** of evidence.

The House of History

Just as a house needs good foundations if it is not to fall down, so a historian needs a sure foundation of **primary sources** if people are going to believe what he writes. Below is a drawing of the House of History with its foundations of primary sources. Try to name other primary and secondary sources for the house.

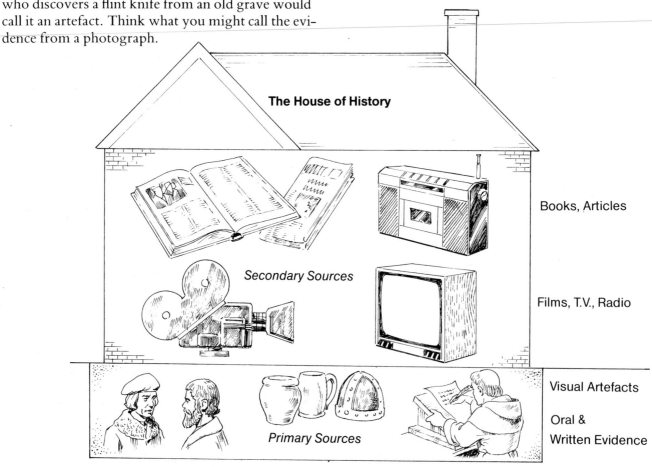

The House of History

Secondary Sources

Books, Articles

Films, T.V., Radio

Visual Artefacts

Oral & Written Evidence

Primary Sources

A Body is Found

Finding your Way in Time

If anyone asks you the time you tell them by looking at your watch or a clock and you say how many hours and minutes have passed in that day. But if you didn't know when time began, just think how difficult it would be to tell how many years, months, days, hours and minutes had passed. Historians sometimes find themselves faced with that problem. They do not know when human history began and they certainly do not know when it will end, and so they are lost somewhere in time. Historians get over this problem by choosing a date on which they all agree and calling it Year 1. In the West the Birth of Christ is chosen as Year 1, and time before this is called Before Christ (BC) and after it Anno Domini (AD) which is the Latin for *'in the year of Our Lord'*. The Romans chose their Year 1 as the year in which Rome was founded. Today Moslems begin their calendar from the Hegira, Thursday 15 July, AD 622, the night Mohammed fled from the city of Mecca. So you see, it does not matter what time you choose to date your calendar from as long as people agree on it.

See if you can place AD 1980, 1980 BC, the Hegira and 55 BC in the time-line below.

Clues in a Silent House

Supposing you visited a strange house in which there was no writing to tell you about the people who lived there. If you were asked to write a story about them you might begin by looking for clues. Photographs might help but you would not know if they were of the people who lived there or if they were taken at the time they were living there. If you found knives and spoons but no forks you might reasonably guess that the people cut up their food and ate it with their fingers or spoons.

Pots, pans and plates would give you an idea of how the people prepared and ate their food. Clothes, or even scraps of cloth, might tell you what these people wore and how they made their materials. The furniture would give you more evidence; for the way in which it was made might give a clue as to when it was made, if you had other furniture with which to compare it. Supposing there were no tables or chairs in the house, you might guess that the people ate their food from dishes set on the floor. Put together, all this evidence would tell you a great deal about how these people lived.

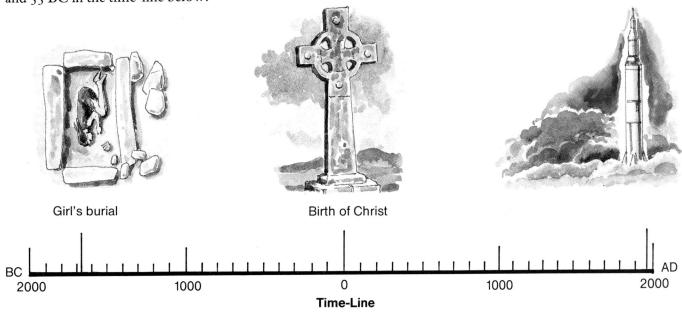

Girl's burial   Birth of Christ

BC   2000   1000   0   1000   2000   AD

Time-Line

Unwritten Prehistory

Many of the sources of evidence that a historian finds are like those in the strange house. They are **unwritten**. As a rough guide the historian calls the time **prehistory** before there was any written evidence. Archaeologists often find much unwritten evidence from which they deduce, or make reasonable guesses about, how people lived. In the same way you might have deduced how the people in the strange house lived by the evidence they left behind them.

Let us look at a real-life mystery and the deductions that were made from it.

A Body is Found

In March 1972 a body was discovered by workmen digging foundations for a Council building-site near Dunfermline. The police were informed and investigations began. The investigators reported the body was that of a young women aged about sixteen. Near the body they found a lighter and a knife with the tip broken off, as well as some other objects. They did not know the cause of death. They thought that the time of death was about 3500 years ago!

As you probably have guessed, the investigators were archaeologists. Below is a drawing of the burial and the things they found in it. Notice that the archaeologists were fairly certain when the girl died. Think where 3500 years ago would fit into your time-line. By knowing roughly when the girl died the archaeologist can fit the burial into his time-line, and compare the things he finds with other artefacts or objects from about the same time. In this way an archaeologist will, in various ways, compare things from the same time without using any kind of written evidence to help him. He or she can then come to certain conclusions about how people lived and died at that time.

Layers of History

When an archaeologist is digging into a site that has been lived in by different groups of people he or she usually deduces that the remains found lower down were left by people who lived there earlier than the people whose remains are on top. This is not always so, for some one later might have disturbed the soil and its remains.

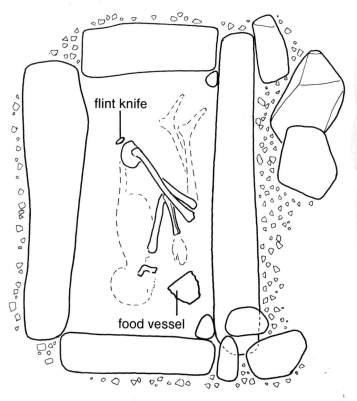

flint knife

food vessel

Let us now look at how the archologists used the objects or artefacts they found in the girl's grave to find out about her and how her tribe lived.

A 'Bronze Age' Burial

Look at the drawing of the grave. The archaeologists found the girl's skeleton lying in a surrounding of stones which they called a **cist**. Next to the skull was a small pot. Beside her waist-bone were a small flint knife with its point broken off, another small piece of flint and a tiny lump of iron ore.

From these few clues the archaeologists were able to work out that the cist was a typical **Bronze Age** burial which dated from about 1630 BC. Bronze is an alloy or mixture of tin and copper. When archaeologists discover artefacts of bronze they know that humans had discovered how to melt metals and then shape or mould them into weapons or tools. But the curious thing was that there were no bronze objects in the girl's grave, and yet the archaeologists called it a 'Bronze Age' burial. Let us see if we can find out the answer to this puzzle. Let us have another look at the grave.

One of the most exciting things to the archaeologists was the fact that the small piece of iron ore and the small piece of flint were so close together. They also guessed that the pot had been used for food and had probably been made by a woman.

Questions and Answers

In many ways the archaeologists were doing a remarkable piece of detective work. Let us see if you can answer some of the questions they asked about the evidence they found. First, they were able to tell that it was a girl's skeleton and not a man's. A dentist was able to tell the archaeologists that from the state of her teeth she had been about sixteen when she died.

Pots

Look at the enlarged drawing below of the pot they found beside the girl's head. Although the archaeologists called it a **food vessel**, it could have contained liquids as well. They were fairly sure it had been made by a woman. If you look closely at the marks around the edge of the pot you will be able to see why the archaeologists thought this. Suppose you had made the pot and had been in a hurry to make these marks on it while the clay was still wet, you would probably have used your finger nails, and those marks were made by *small* fingernails, like those of a woman. Other archaeologists have found similar pots with the marks of grain seeds on their bases—and assumed that these people had already discovered how to grow grain crops. Archaeologists have discovered objects made of bronze alongside this kind of pot. They are therefore able to call the time when these pots were made the Bronze Age. You will be able to find out more about the different 'ages' of mankind in Chapter 2.

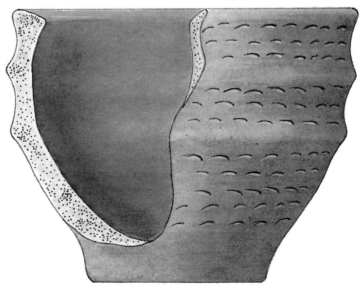

Fire-making

Look at the drawing of the cist again. Remember, the archaeologists were excited when they found a piece of iron ore so near to a small piece of flint. When the girl struck the iron ore with the flint she would get a spark with which she could start a fire. Because they knew when she had died, archaeologists now knew that her tribe had discovered one way of making fires at least 3500 years ago.

Notice how many things we have found out already about the girl's people. We have discovered that they knew how to make pottery, that they probably grew crops and that they knew how to make fire by artificial means.

Graves and Gods

Remember the 'knife'; it could have been used for cutting up food, but the girl could also have used it for cutting skins for clothing. The knife was not a very precious object, and it was certainly not very useful with its point missing. But her tribe had taken great care to put this broken knife into the girl's grave. In many prehistoric graves archaeologists have found swords, spears and other weapons buried alongside kings and chiefs. Sometimes horses, dogs and even people were buried with them. In women's

graves have been found pins, brooches, mirrors and jewellery made of gold and silver. Archaeologists think that these artefacts were buried with the body so that the person's spirit could use them in the after-life. In this way a warrior's spirit would find his best sword, spear and horse all ready to use in his battles in the other world. His wife would also be able to wear her finest ornaments in the next world.

Perhaps then the girl's tribe left these few small objects; the food-vessel with food in it, the knife and her fire-making equipment for her to use after death.

Pictures of the Past

These small objects give us a glimpse of the religious ideas of the girl's tribe. We do not know why the point of the knife was broken; it might have been broken by accident or have been deliberately broken for religious reasons. At other times burial customs changed and the bodies were not buried but burnt and the ashes were placed in special vases or urns. The ways in which customs changed also help archaeologists to date when these burials took place. By putting together the evidence from many thousands of burials all over the world archaeologists are able to gain a better picture of what happened in the past.

Unwritten History

To help them build up a picture of what human life was like before we have written evidence, and help them to date what they find, archaeologists have divided the time which we call **prehistory** into different ages. They name these different ages after the materials from which early people made their implements and weapons. Archaeologists start with the **Old Stone Age** when early people made their implements out of sticks, bones and flint which could be roughly shaped. In the Old Stone Age humans hunted and gathered their food. In the **New Stone Age** they made finer flint tools and weapons. Also at this time they began to herd or 'domesticate' animals such as cattle and sheep. They also began to grow crops and settle in small communities because they no longer needed to follow their prey as it moved to other grazing places. Men, or more likely women, also discovered the way to make fine pottery at this time. The period which followed is called the **Bronze Age** because people found out how to shape implements from bronze. Finally, there came the **Iron Age** when iron was the chief metal for making tools and weapons.

Mixing up the Ages

Although this all sounds neat and simple these different ages are not clearly divided from each other. No one woke up one morning about 2000 BC and said, 'Let's begin the Bronze Age today', and immediately began to make tools out of bronze. Archaeologists think that people began to use tools made of bronze from about 2000 BC onwards in different parts of the world, but others still went on using stone implements. That is why we found stone tools in a girl's grave from the Bronze Age. Sometimes archaeologists even find stone, bronze and iron artefacts in the same grave.

From about c. 13 000 BC to c. 8300 BC most of Britain was covered with glaciers and ice-sheets. (Historians use 'c.' or 'circa' which comes from the Latin *circa* [round about] when they cannot give an exact date to something. You will find 'c.' used a lot when you are reading about prehistory!) The dates c. 13 000–c. 8300 are times of the last Ice Age, or to give it its archaeological name, **Late Last Glacial**.

From c. 8300 to c. 4000 BC the climate grew warmer and wetter. The ice and glaciers began to melt and the level of the seas began to rise. About 6000 to 5000 BC the English Channel was flooded and this cut Britain off from the Continent. Do not imagine that the climate grew warmer during all of this period. At times the weather grew colder and the glaciers and ice would advance again.

The First People in Scotland

People had arrived in Britain before 13 000 BC, but only for short periods to hunt animals. In Scotland archaeologists have discovered some of the earliest human remains at Morton-on-Tay in the north of Fife. They think that these hunters first arrived c. 6000 BC and stayed there off and on until c. 4200 BC in groups of about twelve people for about thirteen days a year. They left some pieces of flint which they had used when making their implements. Bones from animals, such as red deer and voles, and from birds and fish were found at Morton. But because these people lived so near beaches and the mouths of rivers, most of the finds were the remains of shellfish dumped in huge midden heaps.

The Terror of the Sand Dunes

To find out what happened in prehistoric times archaeologists try to piece together the evidence they find. They often have to change their first ideas when they find evidence which does not fit them. We will see how this happened to a famous archaeologist when he excavated a site in Orkney.

The nearest land to the west of Skara Brae in Orkney is Labrador in Canada, nearly 5000 km away. There are no trees at Skara Brae to break the fury of the storms which build up in the Atlantic and can shift the sand-dunes with alarming speed. About 3500 years ago one such storm swept the sands over a village at Skara Brae and the villagers had to flee before they were buried alive. In their haste they left their cooking pots and even the half-eaten remains of their last meal. One woman tried to squeeze through the narrow doorway of her hut in such a hurry that she broke her necklace! After the storm the sand completely covered Skara Brae, sealed it up and preserved it. It was not until AD 1850 that another storm stripped the grass and sand from the buried village. Although a local landowner began to excavate and cleared out four of the huts, it was not until 1927 that a famous archaeologist called V.G. Childe began a proper 'dig' of this perfectly preserved Stone Age village.

Archaeological 'Digs'

Do not let the word 'dig' mislead you. Nowadays when archaeologists start a dig they uncover the site with great care. As they remove the earth or sand they examine each layer carefully and any objects which they find are labelled and recorded on a plan of the dig. Each object is carefully cleaned and preserved. Then archaeologists write a description of it, saying how old they think it is, what it is made of and what it might have been used for. Notice how often the word 'care' has been used, for archaeologists know that once they start a dig they will never be able to restore the site to the condition in which they found it. They cannot replace the objects where they

discovered them because they wish to preserve them in some safe place to enable other archaeologists to examine them. So you see the dig will 'destroy' the site, and this makes it very important for archaeologists to record exactly what they do for anyone coming after them.

The pictures on this page show you how digs were carried out years ago and what a modern excavation looks like. In the old dig the searcher just dug into the site and made no attempt to record each new layer of finds. Nowadays, great care is taken and everything is carefully measured and recorded.

One of the huts at Skara Brae after excavation.

The Dig at Skara Brae

At Skara Brae, Childe discovered the remains of ten circular huts buried under the sand and midden-rubbish from the huts. He thought the huts had been built at different times. Everything was built of stone, not only the walls but the beds, cupboards, 'dressers' and doorposts. Around the outside of the walls the villagers had piled all their rubbish. Although part of the roofs had been made of whalebones and perhaps wood, why do you think the buildings and their contents were mostly made of stone? Under a wall the bodies of two women were found and Childe thought they had been placed there for some religious reason.

Strange Stones

In some of the later houses Childe found round stones with knobs. He was not very sure what they had been used for, but later archaeologists think they were per-

haps used when the villagers met to discuss matters which involved the whole tribe. At these meetings the stones would be passed to the next person to speak and everyone would listen to him or her.

Midden Heaps

Midden heaps do not sound very exciting, but they told Childe a great deal about the life the villagers led. In them he found thousands of pieces of bones from cattle, sheep and other animals such as wild pig. There was also a great number of limpet shells.

Water Tanks

In all the houses Childe found hearth stones which had been used for fires. Some houses had stone tanks lined with clay, and Childe thought the villagers might have kept limpets in them as well as water.

'Pastoralists'

Childe called these people 'pastoralists' because they herded animals. Notice he didn't call them 'hunters' as he found no evidence to show that they tracked down and killed animals. Later archaeologists found some whalebones which they thought might have been used for pounding corn and so the villagers may also have grown cereals.

The First Villagers

Childe could not answer one important question: when had the first people arrived at Skara Brae? However, at a village called Rinyo near Skara Brae another archaeologist found an important clue. The huts at Rinyo were built in the same way as the oldest ones at Skara Brae and contained the same kinds of objects. But something else was found as well—a beaker.

This discovery made Childe think hard. He had assumed that Skara Brae and Rinyo had originally been settled during the first few centuries BC, long after the people who had made Beaker Pottery. But if a beaker was found among examples of the local pottery made at Rinyo, and Skara Brae had been sealed

off at an early date, then the first villagers at Skara Brae must have lived there at or before the time the Beaker People had arrived. What made this discovery even more exciting was that the local type of pottery —not beakers—at Rinyo was very similar to pottery found at Clacton-on-Sea in Essex. This meant that the people in Rinyo were perhaps related in some way to people from the South of England.

Childe also found other connections between the Orkney settlements and Clacton. You will remember the strange stones he had found at Skara Brae; he found more of them at Rinyo, and both finds were similar to those found at Clacton. At Rinyo he also found sticks which he thought had been used for digging the ground, and so he deduced that the people at Rinyo had carried out a simple way of growing crops. Sickles were found at Clacton which looks as though the wide-spread Rinyo-Clacton people had discovered how to plant, grow and harvest crops.

Childe wrote that people from Skara Brae and Rinyo belonged to the **Neolithic** period of prehistory. Neolithic means 'New Stone Age' and you will remember from the beginning of this chapter that this age was a time of great changes in human history.

How Civilization Spread

In Childe's time an archaeologist had no sure way of dating prehistoric remains. Childe had the idea that all the discoveries which made the New Stone Age so different—the growing of crops and the domestication of animals—had begun in the river-valleys of the Nile in Egypt and the Tigris and Euphrates in modern Iraq. He believed that these methods of farming had gradually spread or 'diffused' from these river-valleys in the Middle East across Europe to Britain. He called this idea the 'Diffusionist Theory'.

This is a reconstruction of the pot found at Rinyo. Notice how few fragments were actually found.

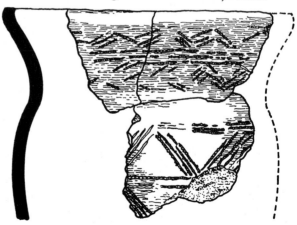

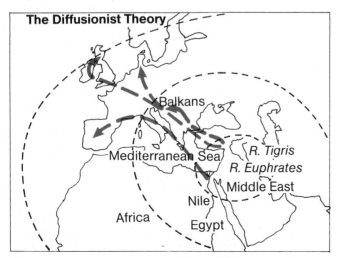

The Diffusionist Theory

Balkans

Mediterranean Sea

R. Tigris

R. Euphrates

Middle East

Nile

Africa

Egypt

Remember the beaker that was found at Rinyo. It might have been used for drinking a kind of ale, perhaps made of barley. Archaeologists have worked out that the people who made these beakers came to Britain c. 2000 BC. They think that the Beaker People came first from Spain and Northern France and settled over a wide area in Western Europe, for their beakers have been found in places as far apart as Sicily and Poland. In Holland and the mouth of the river Rhine they seem to have been joined by other tribes who used stone axes as weapons. About 2000 BC the Beaker People crossed the North Sea to Britain, and in Scotland their remains have been found at different places on the East coast from Aberdeen to the River Tweed. The Beaker People brought new ways of making things with them. Above all, they had discovered how to make bronze.

They also brought with them many new ideas. Earlier tribes had usually buried their chiefs and other important people together in long, stone-lined tombs which were covered with earth. These tombs are called 'barrows' by archaeologists. When the Beaker People buried one of their tribe they placed the body in a separate cist, sometimes with a stone 'lid' covered with earth. You will remember how the girl was buried in *Case History 1: A Body Is Found* and the position of the girl's body. This was the usual way of burying women's bodies among the Beaker People.

An Iron Age smith

Archaeologists now think that the Bronze Age, which started with the coming of the Beaker People, lasted until c. 600 BC. Then new tribes of people who used iron for their tools and implements began to arrive in Britain. You will read about these new people in the next chapter.

Getting the Dates Right

When Childe wrote about Skara Brae in 1927–30 he said that the first settlement there dated from the New Stone Age and could be dated 'as late as 300 BC'. In other words he could not give a definite date. By 1972 when archaeologists examined the girl's grave they were much more confident about the time of her burial for they said she had died 40 years before or after 1631 BC. Between 1927 and 1972, therefore, great changes had taken place in the ways in which archaeologists were able to date prehistoric remains (as you will see in *Case History 2*).

Something to Remember

This chapter shows how archaeologists have divided up the dating of prehistory. These are very rough dates based on the materials that people used for making tools and implements. The Old Stone Age was a period when artefacts were made roughly out of stone, usually of flint which could be chipped to form sharp edges. The New Stone Age is a period of great changes. Stone implements were more skilfully made, but the most important changes were when man began to grow crops and domesticate animals. The Bronze Age in Britain saw the coming of the Beaker People c. 2000 BC. Finally, the last 'metal' age, that of Iron, was when the Celts began to arrive in this country about 600 BC. Archaeologists break these different ages up to show when new ways of doing things started, such as making pottery. In this way we can have periods like **Late Bronze Age** or **Mesolithic** (Middle Stone Age).

It is important to remember that these different ages did not begin everywhere at the same time. If Childe's 'diffusion' theory is correct, it could have taken hundreds of years for new techniques to travel from the Middle East to this country. Also, the different ages merge into one another so that we find stone artefacts in 'Bronze Age' burials.

Notice how careful archaeologists have to be when they are excavating. Once a site has been dug it can never be restored to its original state. This means that archaeologists must keep details of everything that they find and where it was found. They must be able to change their ideas if they discover something unexpected. Childe had to revise his ideas about the age of Skara Brae when a beaker was found at a similar site at Rinyo.

Something to Think About

This chapter shows us how we must be able to change our ideas if we are going to progress. Some ideas are easy to change. If a new way of making fire or computers is discovered people usually make changes quite quickly because the advantages are fairly obvious. But there are some changes which we find difficult to make. For hundreds of years people thought the world was flat and it took a long time before they changed their mind—in fact some still believe in the earth's flatness.

This chapter shows how archaeology is exciting because archaeologists must be able to change even their deepest-felt ideas if new evidence comes along. It does not mean that archaeologists are constantly changing their minds. But it does mean that they have to consider each new piece of evidence; they have to be able to change or reshape some of their ideas.

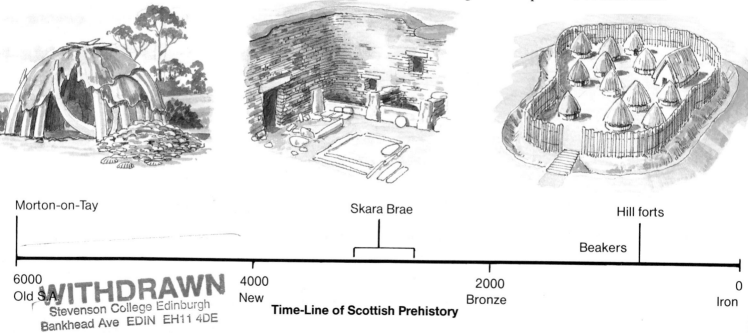

Morton-on-Tay   Skara Brae   Hill forts

Beakers

| 6000 | | 4000 | | 2000 | 0 |
| Old S.A. | | New | | Bronze | Iron |

Time-Line of Scottish Prehistory

Science Tells the Time

Through his knowledge of pottery and other artefacts Childe was able to say that his finds at Skara Brae dated from the New Stone Age. He might have given them a date but we have seen how wrong he could be. In other words, he was guessing. For example, if an archaeologist is lucky enough to find a coin in a grave with the head of a ruler on it, and knows that the ruler began reigning in 100 BC, then he or she can be fairly sure that the body had been buried some time after 100 BC. Notice, the archaeologist can only be *fairly sure* because someone might have put the coin into a much earlier grave. It would not be possible to tell *how long after* 100 BC the burial had taken place from the coin for the buried person's family might have kept the coin as a souvenir for generations. But if the burial had happened before c.650 BC, when the first real coins were made in Asia Minor, modern Turkey, the archaeologist would not have been able to use coins to date any finds.

Tree Rings

American archaeologists who were excavating the remains of Indian villages in the south-west of the United States discovered one method of dating their finds. As you probably know, a tree grows by adding a ring to its trunk each year. The width of the ring depends upon the climate; if the climate is good then the ring will be wide, if it is bad then the tree will only add a narrow ring. The archaeologists noticed how changes in the climate left tell-tale patterns in the tree-rings. The hot, dry, desert climate had preserved the timber which the Indians had used for building their houses. By comparing the tree-rings of the timbers with a living tree, when a living tree had been used in building a house, the archaeologists were able to tell when the houses were built. Then by counting the patterns of the rings right up to the present day they were able to date accurately when the timbers from any house had been used. The diagram below shows you how the tree-ring method of dating works. But remember, this method will work better with timbers that have been perserved by a dry climate.

Tree-ring dating

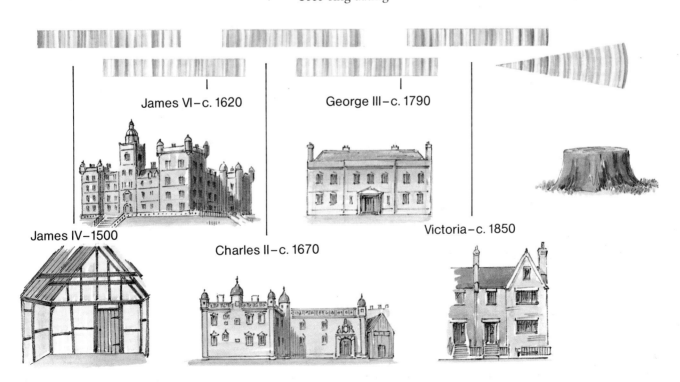

James VI–c. 1620

George III–c. 1790

James IV–1500

Charles II–c. 1670

Victoria–c. 1850

Radio-Active Archaeology

All living creatures, whether they are animal or vegetable, contain the chemical element Carbon. In fact, there are two kinds of Carbon, Carbon 12 and Carbon 14. Carbon 14, (C14), is radio-active. The proportions of the two Carbons remain constant to each other while the creature is still alive. As soon as the creature dies the amount of C14 begins to decrease, *at a steady rate*, while the amount of C12 remains the same. Scientists have found out that only half the original amount of C14 remains after roughly 5730 years—this is called the 'half-life' of C14. William Libby, an American scientist, invented a method by which he could tell how much C14 remained in bones, wood or seeds which had been found in a dig. In this way he could tell roughly when the animal or plant had died. As it is very difficult to work out *exactly* how much Carbon 14 still exists in any specimen, archaeologists add a plus or minus number of years to their Carbon 14 (C14) dates. That is why the archaeologists wrote that the girl in *Case History 1* had died in 1631 BC plus or minus 40 years.

Archaeologists now had a much more accurate way of dating the past, and C14 dating produced some very surprising results for the dates in British prehistory. Before C14 it was generally accepted among archaeologists that the New Stone Age in Britain had begun about 2500 BC. It soon became clear after C14 tests that this date was much too late—by about a thousand years. This means that the New Stone Age began c.3500 BC.

The use of C14 for dating does not mean that archaeologists are completely certain about dates in prehistoric times. Sometimes objects from the same place in a dig come up with different C14 dates. Archaeologists and scientists believe that the amount of radio-activity in the atmosphere may have varied at different times. They are also worried at the extent to which archaeological finds might have become 'contaminated' by our atmosphere today after all the atomic tests which have been carried out since 1945. So the search will continue for new ways of finding out about the past. But one thing is certain—the archaeologist will learn more and more from the scientist.

Carbon 14 dating

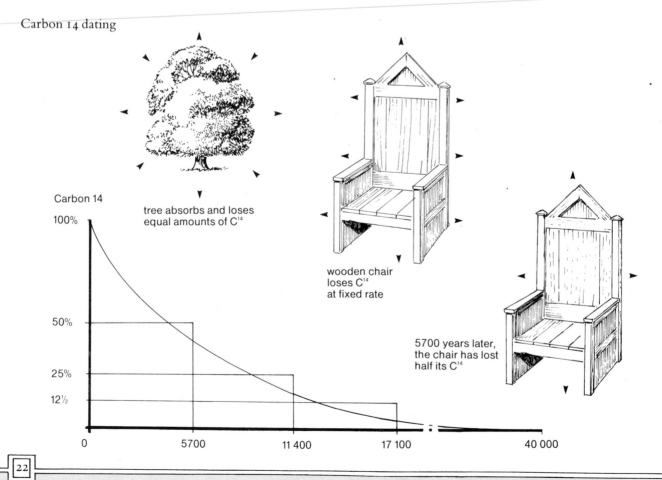

tree absorbs and loses equal amounts of C¹⁴

wooden chair loses C¹⁴ at fixed rate

5700 years later, the chair has lost half its C¹⁴

Carbon 14

100%

50%

25%

12½

0   5700   11 400   17 100   40 000

Our Celtic Inheritance

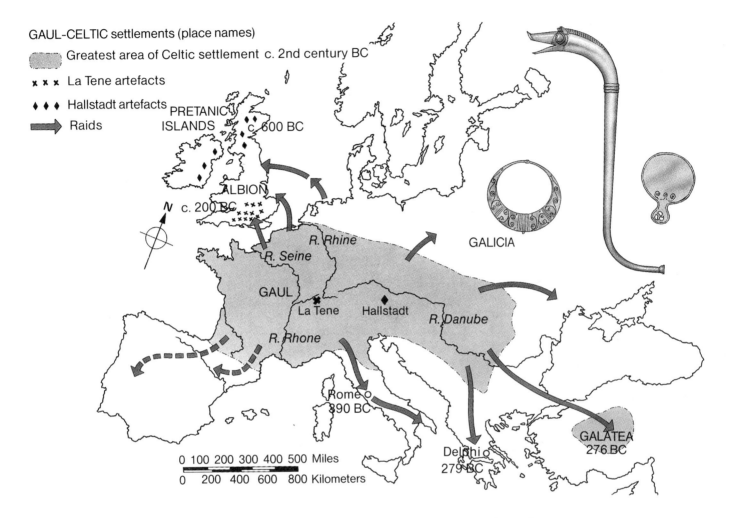

GAUL-CELTIC settlements (place names)

Greatest area of Celtic settlement c. 2nd century BC

x x x La Tene artefacts

♦ ♦ ♦ Hallstadt artefacts

→ Raids

PRETANIC ISLANDS
c. 600 BC
ALBION c. 200 BC
N
R. Rhine
R. Seine
GAUL
La Tene   Hallstadt
R. Rhone
R. Danube
GALICIA
Rome 890 BC
Delphi 279 BC
GALATEA 276 BC

0 100 200 300 400 500 Miles
0 200 400 600 800 Kilometers

In Chapter 1 we saw how John's great-grandfather left evidence of the years when he was a soldier. We have also seen lots of different kinds of evidence that prehistoric people have left us. Sometimes people in the past leave us more than a few bones or artefacts.

One race of people, called the Celts, who came to Scotland about 3000 years ago at the start of the Iron Age, left behind traces of themselves which still remain with us today. In parts of Scotland people still speak Gaelic, a Celtic language. Hallowe'en night was feared by the Celts for then, they believed, evil spirits roamed about. At Christmas we often use mistletoe, a plant sacred to the Celts. In fact, traces of the Celts are still with us in many ways. Let us now see who these Celts were and where they came from; how they lived and what else they have handed down to us.

Celtic Civilisation

A Greek writer called Posidonius wrote this about the Celts in the first century BC:

> The whole race which is now called Gallic is madly fond of war, high-spirited and quick to battle, but otherwise straightfoward and not of evil character.

Posidonius, like other Greek and Roman writers, calls the Celts 'Gauls'.

As you can see from the map above, the first tribes known as Celts came from north and west of the Alps. They began to move across Europe after 1000 BC. Wherever they went they impressed people with their bravery and fierce fighting. This is how one

Celtic warrior challenged Cuchulainn, the greatest of all Celtic heroes:

> I have come, a wild boar of the herd . . . to thrust you beneath the waters of the pool. . . . Here is the one who will crush you. It is I who will slay you, for it is I who can.

His boasting didn't do him much good for Cuchulainn cut him in three pieces with two blows!

In 390 BC the Gauls besieged Rome and a legend tells us how the city was only saved by the sacred geese who gave the Romans warning of a night attack by the Gauls. The Celts invaded Greece. Some travelled even further east into Turkey. The Celts who attacked Rome came from the land which the Romans later called 'Gaul' and which included modern France, Belgium, Switzerland and the Rhineland.

The Greeks and Romans thought the Celts were barbarians. But as the Greeks thought that anyone who did not speak their language or know Greek customs was a barbarian, this must not lead us into thinking that the Celts were uncivilised. The Celts had their own language and customs and gods. They fashioned beautiful things out of gold and silver. In many ways they were as skilful as the Romans and Greeks in their use of these metals. They were fierce, boastful and liked drinking; but they were not uncivilised.

The Iron Age

The first Celts cremated their dead and placed their ashes in urns made of clay. Between 700 BC and 600 BC this burial custom changed among the chiefs and other important people. In these new burials the body was laid out unburnt with all its possessions on a four-wheeled cart. The most important change in these burials is that the weapons are made of iron instead of bronze. These changes make up what archaeologists call the Hallstadt culture from the village in Austria where a large number of these burials were found last century.

By c. 500 BC the centre of Celtic power seems to have shifted to 'Gaul' from Central Europe. This period is famous for the beautiful Celtic metal-work called La Tene after a lake in Switzerland in which large numbers of ornaments had been thrown as offerings to the gods.

The Celts in Britain

The appearance of the Celts in Britain about 650 BC is marked by the building of many 'hill-forts'. Archaeologists think they were built by the Celtic incomers and by the tribes who were here before them. These hill-forts were not only used to defend tribes against attacks, sometimes they were just small settlements with banks of earth in which cattle were corralled. These earlier Celts spoke a language called 'Goidelic' which is the ancestor of Scottish and Irish Gaelic. (Notice too how close 'Gaul' and 'Gael' are.)

About 100 BC large numbers of another Celtic tribe, the Belgae, came from Northern Gaul to south-east England. They kept their contacts with the Continental Belgae and gave them help against the Roman invasions. This may have been one of the reasons why Julius Caesar launched his invasion of England in 55 BC. These later arrivals spoke 'Brythonic' Celtic from which modern Welsh and the Breton language of Brittany come. Notice where the name 'Briton' comes from.

Celts of the Halstadt culture may have reached north-east Scotland as early as 600 BC. By the first century BC the south of Scotland seems to have been settled by tribes speaking Brythonic Celtic. Some of the 'Scottish' Britons may have come from England, such as the Dumnonii of central Scotland who were related to the Dumnonii of south-west England. These Celts who settled on the coastal plains north of the Forth, perhaps they were mainly warriors, mixed with the original people there. This mixture of people was called *Caledonii* or *Picti* by the Romans.

New Kinds of Evidence

If you read the description of the Celts by Posidonius again, you will see the new kind of evidence he gives us. In the last chapter we were looking at **unwritten** evidence but now Posidonius gives us **written** evidence. Written history can tell us much, but a historian needs to read this kind of evidence very carefully. The early Celts left us no writing and so we have to rely for most of our information about them from Greek and Roman writers. Supposing Posidonius had been a great enemy of the Celts, think whether it would have made any difference to what he wrote, whether it would have changed what we know about them. Remember, too, that Posidonius is a **primary** source because he was living at the same

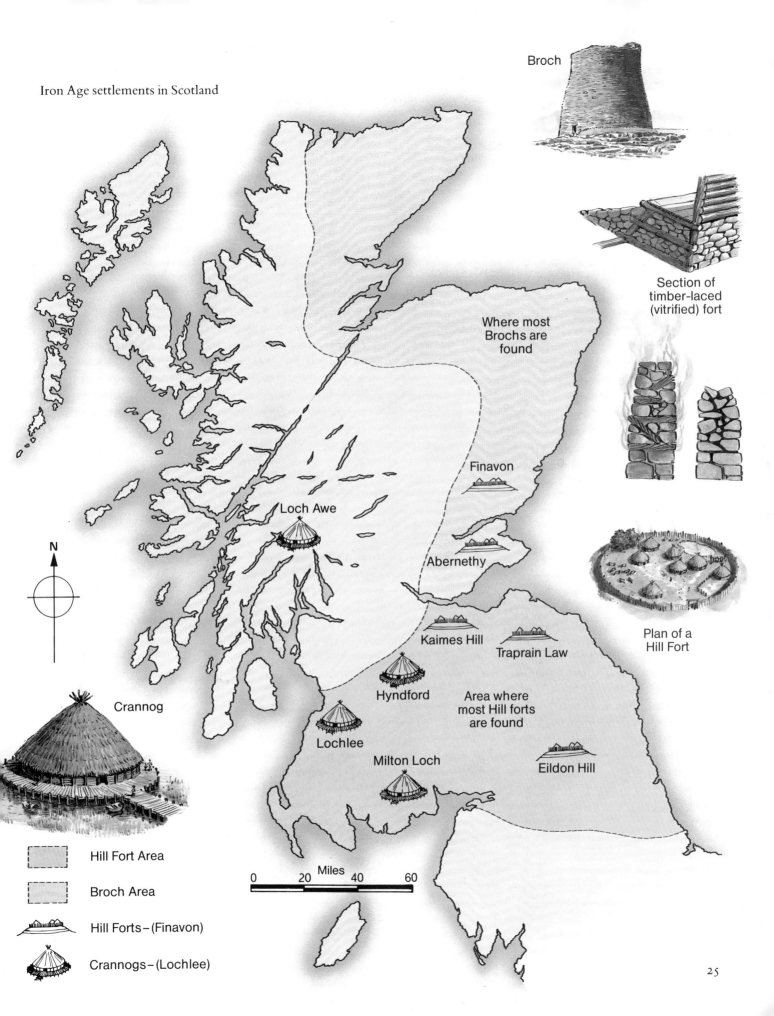

Iron Age settlements in Scotland

Broch

Section of timber-laced (vitrified) fort

Where most Brochs are found

Finavon

Loch Awe

Abernethy

N

Plan of a Hill Fort

Kaimes Hill

Traprain Law

Hyndford

Area where most Hill forts are found

Lochlee

Milton Loch

Eildon Hill

Crannog

Miles
0   20   40   60

Hill Fort Area

Broch Area

Hill Forts–(Finavon)

Crannogs–(Lochlee)

25

time as the Celts he was writing about. Think what we would have to do if we had *two* primary sources with differing opinions about the Celts. This is one of most difficult things for anyone reading about the past to make up his or her mind about.

Place Names

You have already seen some of the clues that people in the past leave after them. Place names can also give us clues about the people who once stayed there. The Romans called the Celts 'Gauls', and places where they settled often have the word 'Gal—' in them. 'Gaul' is one, but there are many others scattered about Europe—even in Turkey there was once a region called 'Galatia'. Finally a reminder, think of the name of the Celtic language still spoken in Scotland.

Hill-forts

Earlier we saw that many hill-forts seem to have been built when the Celts first appeared in Britain. These forts are found all over Europe where the Celts settled. There are hill-forts in most parts of Scotland, but mostly in the south and east. The photograph below is of the remains of one of these sites, at Braidwood in Midlothian.

They are about 40 acres (16h.) in size. Some of them were much larger—about the size of a small town and so are called **oppida** which is the Latin word for towns. One of the largest oppida in Scotland was on Traprain Law in East Lothian where a great treasure was found in 1919. But there were even larger oppida in England and on the Continent. Inside the hill-forts the wooden huts were circular.

Glass forts

Between the River Tay and the Great Glen are many 'glass' or **vitrified** forts. They receive this strange name as their walls have a glassy appearance. Archaeologists think that timber was interlaced in the stone walls to give them strength. At some time the timbers were set on fire and the great heat melted the stones. When the stones cooled they were smooth and glassy. Their name comes from the Latin word for glass, *vitrum*. It is not known if the occupants set fire to the walls deliberately to make them even stronger or if the fires were started by enemies.

Brochs

The picture above is an artist's impression of a most remarkable kind of fort which is only seen in Scotland. This type is called a **broch** and is found mostly in the north-east, the Orkney and Shetland Isles. Most brochs are in places settled by the Picts, many of them being built near the coast where they were perhaps used as defence against attacks by enemies from the sea.

Brochs are always circular and made like dry-stone dykes. The two walls are 'tied' together by long stones which lend them strength. The space between the walls was used for living space as well as for stairs to the top of the broch. The walls were very tall: the one at Mousa in Shetland is still over 40 feet (12m.) high.

Early archaeologists were attracted to the brochs which seemed very romantic buildings to them. Unfortunately for those who came later, the early digs were carried out very badly and little was left for later excavators. This made it very difficult to tell when the brochs were occupied. The discovery of a few Roman coins made archaeologists think they had been built in the first two centuries AD. However, in 1978 a dig at a newly found broch at Bu, near Stromness, made archaeologists rethink their dates. Carbon 14 dating showed finds from c.600 BC, nearly 500 years earlier than archaeologists had thought.

Water Forts

In their search for safety some tribes built an artificial island in the middle of a loch. They probably floated out a raft of logs and then piled it with stones until it sank. They would repeat this until an 'island' appeared and they would then build their huts on top. Most of these 'crannogs' or lake-dwellings have been found in the south of Scotland. A large crannog at Milton Loch in Kirkcudbrightshire has given a C14 date of AD 490 plus or minus 100 years. Though the crannogs must have been fairly safe from attack they must also have been very damp and uncomfortable when the level of the loch rose.

Gods and Priests

The gods of the Celts were poets, warriors, law-givers and doctors for these were the kind of people the Celts admired. One of their chief gods, Dagda, was good and immensely strong. He carried a club and owned a cauldron which always had enough food for anyone who ate from it. Dagda was married to a goddess who could turn herself into a horse, an animal the Celts admired, for their chief warriors fought on horseback or used chariots. Cernunnos was admired and feared by the Celts for he was 'The Lord of the Beasts' and had power over all animals. The picture of Cernunnos above is on a silver cauldron from Denmark. It shows the god with his antlers surrounded by animals. He grasps a snake with his left hand and holds his sacred torc or neck-band in his right. Like all the Celtic gods, Cernunnos could change his shape at will.

Like some of us, the Celts thought three was a lucky number. Many of them worshipped the same three-headed god whose statues have been found in Britain, France and Germany. They also thought some trees were sacred, especially the oak tree on which the holy mistletoe grew. A Roman historian called Pliny wrote:

> They [the Celts] call the mistletoe by a name that means 'all-healing' . . . and it is an antidote for all poisons.

Why do you think people kiss under the mistletoe?

Druids

The Druids who were the priests of the Celts regarded the oak tree as holy. The Celtic druids were not like the modern druids who meet at Stonehenge on Midsummer's Day, or at the Welsh Eisteddfod. They were poets and prophets who were supposed to possess great magical powers. A druid would judge quarrels and arguments, and even a king would not interrupt a druid when he was speaking. It took a man twenty years of hard study to become a druid for he had to remember everything, as the druids did not write down their sacred knowledge.

Celtic Time

The druids would preside over the ceremonies which took place four times a year. The Celts did not reckon their time in days but by nights. In this way their calendar was based on moon-months. A season began on Beltane Night, 1 May, and on that night the Celts drove their cattle between two rows of fire to purify them. You may know of places in Scotland where Beltane Fairs are still held today. August 1st was a harvest feast held in honour of the the god, Lugh. The night of 31 October, Samain, was the beginning of the Celtic New Year, a very dangerous time for mortals. On that night, between the Old and New Years, the spirits of the dead roamed freely. Then the raven, the bird of death, was to be seen with other evil spirits—think of what happens on 31 October nowadays. Finally, 1 February was the goddess Brigit's night and when the Celts became Christians that date became St Brigid's feast day.

Warriors

The Celts and Romans fought each other for centuries. Though the Romans finally conquered Gaul and most of Britain they admired the courage of the Celtic warriors. The Celts' favourite weapon was the long sword made of iron which they used for cutting and slashing. They also used spears for throwing and stabbing. The Celtic poets often tell us how the warriors loved to fight man to man as this would give greater glory to the victor. In Britain their greatest warriors fought from chariots, as Julius Caesar found to his surprise when he invaded in 55 BC:

> This is the manner of fighting from war chariots. First they drive along throwing their spears, and by the terror caused by the horses and the noise of the wheels they generally succeed in throwing into confusion the ranks of the enemy.

If a warrior killed a foe in battle he would cut off his opponent's head and take it back to his hut where he would proudly nail it to the door-post. A warrior would boast of the number of heads he and his ancestors had taken in this way and:

> some of them would boast that they refused the weight of the head in gold

from the families of the dead men. You can understand why the Romans feared to fall into Celtic hands!

The Monster of Noves.
He is holding the heads of
two victims in his claws.

The Appearance of Celts

Greek and Roman writers were impressed by the appearance of the Celts. They described them as tall and muscular, with white skins and long, fair hair. Here is a picture of a statue called the 'Dying Gaul' by a Greek sculptor. The warrior is meeting his death bravely and with dignity.

> Almost all the Gauls are of tall stature, fair and ruddy, terrible for the fierceness of their eyes.

The men often shaved their beards and allowed their moustaches to grow over their mouths. Again Posidonius tells us how they wore:

> ornaments of gold, torcs on their necks and bracelets on their ams and wrists.

They were very proud, even vain, about how they looked. Unlike the men of the Mediterranean countries who wore robes, the Celts wore trousers and a tunic belted at the waist. Over this they wore a cloak and the richness of this showed the importance of its owner. You will find out what happened when these proud, brave but unorganised warriors met the well-disciplined might of the Roman legions in the next *Case History*.

Something to Remember

The Celts get their name from the language they spoke and which they have left to their descendants today in languages like Gaelic and Welsh. The first signs that they had developed a 'Celtic' culture different from their neighbours appear about 1200 BC. By c.800 BC archaeologists can see a 'Hallstadt' culture which spreads to cover much of Western Europe.

In Britain the coming of the Celts is marked by the appearance of hill-forts. These hill-forts differ greatly in size, ranging from large 'oppida' to a cluster of huts. In Scotland we have hill-forts, called 'vitrified' forts, and brochs which are found only in his country. This beginning of the Iron Age is thought to have been a time of many tribal wars.

Celtic religion is still with us in some ways. We celebrate Hallowe'en, and May Day is still a popular festival.

The Celts were fierce, brave and barbaric but they were not uncivilised. Their art still influences artists, especially those who use metal. Their stories about their heroes and gods were passed on by word of mouth until they were written down by Christian monks, the descendants of these Celts.

Something to Think About

In this chapter we find the first written sources being used. As they were written by Greeks and Romans about the Celts we will have to be careful how much we can rely on them. Such written evidence is often full of the writer's opinions. It can also be 'biased', i.e. the evidence can be one-sided, or lean heavily to one side or the other. As historians rely on written evidence a great deal it means that they have to be extremely careful about how much weight they give to any piece of written evidence.

The Romans in Scotland

The first person living in Scotland whose name we know was Calgacus. His Celtic name meant 'the swordsman' and he was the leader of a Caledonian army defeated by the Romans in AD 83 at the battle of Mons Graupius. The question is: what were the soldiers of the mighty Roman Empire doing in such a remote corner of Europe?

Many of you will remember that Julius Caesar landed near Dover in 55 BC. This landing and the next in the following year were only raids, not invasions. Nearly 100 years later, however, in AD 43, the Romans returned under the Emperor Claudius and conquered most of modern England in the next few years. The Romans, like the British in India over 1700 years later, found out that in order to protect their conquests they had to wage war against the fierce tribes who lived to the north. Therefore, in AD 80 the Roman Governor, Agricola, decided to conquer the Celtic and Caledonian tribes who lived to the north of York and Chester, as they were a threat to the Roman peace.

Agricola

Agricola had become Governor of Roman Britain in AD 78. We know more about Agricola's invasion of Scotland than any other Roman campaign against tribes on the Roman frontier. This is because his biography, or life-story, was written by his son-in-law, Tacitus. Tacitus greatly admired Agricola so, of course, we must be very careful when we read him. Many of the things Tacitus wrote about Agricola's invasion of Caledonia, however, have been confirmed by archaeologists.

Between 80 and 81 Agricola pushed northwards as far as the River Tay, where he stopped. As Tacitus writes:

> a good place for halting the advance was found in Britain itself. The Clyde and the Forth, carried inland to a great depth on the tides of opposite seas, are separated only by a narrow neck of land. This isthmus was now firmly held by garrisons, and the whole expanse of country to the south was safely in our hands. The enemy had been pushed into what was virtually another island.

In his later campaigns Agricola advanced northwards on the eastern side of Scotland, carefully avoiding possible dangers from the Highland glens.

'They Create a Desolation and Call It Peace'

In 83 he fought the battle of Mons Graupius with the Caledonians. Historians have not yet located the battlefield, though some say it was near Keith in Banffshire, and a strong case has been made out for Durno in Aberdeenshire. Before the battle, Tacitus writes, Calgacus had stirred up the courage of his men when he had said this about the Romans:

> They [the Romans] are the only people to whose covetousness [greed] both riches and poverty are equally tempting. To robbery, butchery and rapine [rape] they give the lying name of 'government'; they create a desolation [desert] and call it peace.

Later, Calgacus added:

> Which will you choose—to follow your leader into battle, or to submit to taxation, labour in the mines, and all the other tribulations [hardships] of slavery?

Remember, this is Tacitus writing and he knew how the Romans treated the people they had conquered. Perhaps he was trying to tell the Romans that if they continued in this cruel fashion they would make undying enemies of the conquered.

Tacitus writes that the Romans lost only 360 soldiers and killed 10 000 Caledonians. Let Tacitus take up the story:

> The next day revealed the effects of our victory more fully. An awful silence reigned on every hand; the hills were deserted, houses smoking in the distance, and our scouts did not meet a soul.

CASE HISTORY

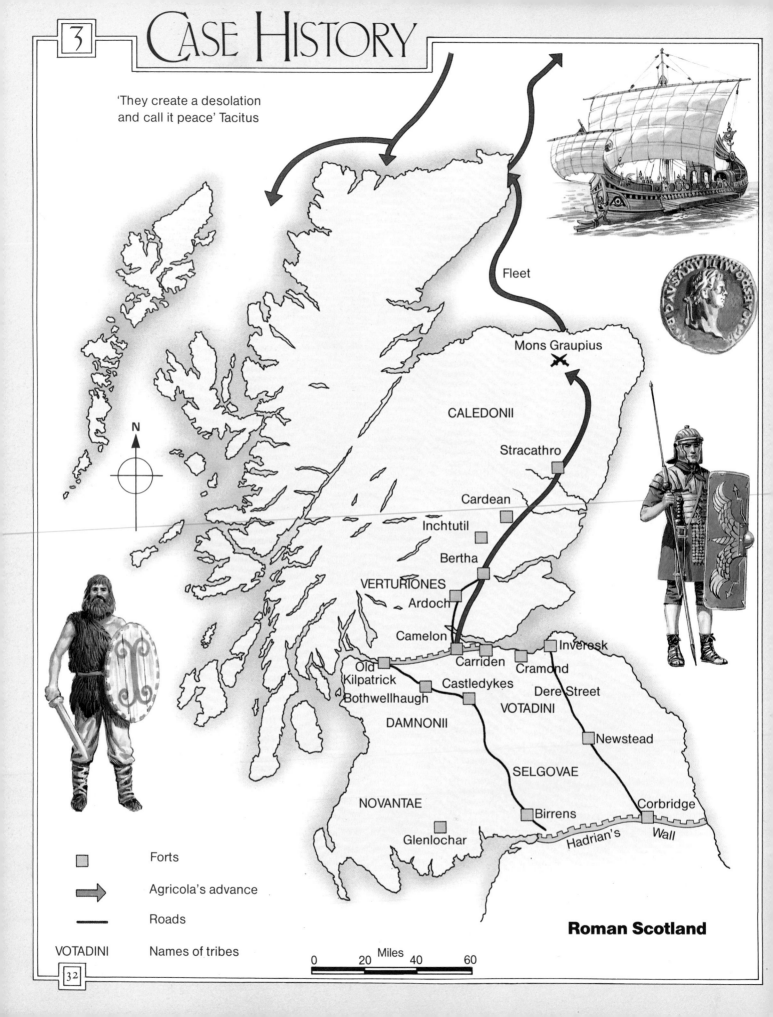

'They create a desolation
and call it peace' Tacitus

Fleet

Mons Graupius ✗

CALEDONII

Stracathro ◻

Cardean ◻

Inchtutil ◻

Bertha ◻

VERTURIONES

Ardoch ◻

Camelon ◻

Carriden ◻   Inveresk ◻

Old
Kilpatrick ◻   Cramond

Castledykes ◻   Dere Street

Bothwellhaugh   VOTADINI

DAMNONII

Newstead ◻

SELGOVAE

NOVANTAE   Corbridge ◻

Birrens ◻   Wall

Glenlochar ◻   Hadrian's

N

◻ Forts

➔ Agricola's advance

— Roads

VOTADINI   Names of tribes

Miles

0   20   40   60

Roman Scotland

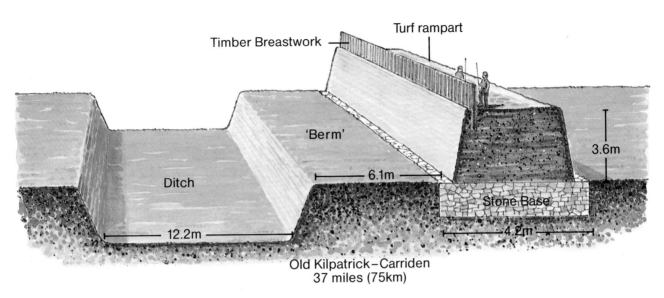

Timber Breastwork — Turf rampart

'Berm'

3.6m

Ditch

6.1m

12.2m

Stone Base

4.2m

Old Kilpatrick–Carriden
37 miles (75km)

A section through the Antonine Wall

The Purpose of the Roman Forts

The Romans, according to Tacitus, had won a great victory. It was very likely that a large part of the Caledonian warriors escaped death or capture, including Calgacus, otherwise Tacitus would have been sure to have mentioned something that would have given greater glory to Agricola.

Although he had defeated the Caledonians Agricola did not push on with his conquest. Instead, he built a line of forts stretching from Drymen in Stirlingshire to Stracathro in Angus. Historians disagree about Agricola's reasons for building these forts. Some say that they were built at the mouths of the Highland glens to prevent the Caledonians attacking the newly-conquered territory. Other historians say that they were built as 'glen-stoppers', but for the opposite reason, *to stop the newly-conquered Caledonians from escaping up the glens*. Remember what Calgacus, or rather Tacitus, had said about slavery.

Within twenty years the Romans had withdrawn from Scotland to a line of forts between the English River Tyne and Solway Bay. Perhaps the Romans did not consider Scotland rich enough to hold on to, and they certainly needed soldiers to fight on the Continent. In AD 122 the Emperor Hadrian ordered his men to build the wall that is named after him between Newcastle and Carlisle. Maybe this wall was built for the same purposes as Agricola's forts.

The Longest Wall in Scotland

Then, nearly twenty years later, another Roman army marched north of Hadrian's Wall. This time they built the longest wall ever seen in Scotland, nearly 40 miles (64 km) long, running from Carriden near Bo'ness on the Forth to Old Kilpatrick on the Clyde. This wall ran along the line of Agricola's earlier forts between the two rivers.

The Romans called it the Antonine Wall after their Emperor Antoninus Pius who:

> conquered the Britons through Lollius Urbicus, the Governor, and after driving back the barbarians, built another wall, this time of turf.

We are not sure why the Romans launched this new invasion. There had been trouble on both sides of Hadrian's Wall and the Emperor had decided to push all the trouble-makers behind a new wall. Also he was not a soldier and perhaps wanted a cheap victory to give him the title 'Imperator' (Conqueror). Notice how the conquest was carried out 'through' Lollius Urbicus.

Roman Carvings

The slab on this page was found in 1868 at Bridgeness in West Lothian. Roughly translated it says:

> In the reign of the Emperor Antoninus Pius the II Legion August put up this slab to mark the building of 4652 feet [1420m] of wall.

The left-hand side shows a Roman cavalryman killing a Caledonian, while another is trampled under his horse's hooves. A third Caledonian has been taken prisoner, and a fourth has been beheaded. Think of where you have read of this custom before and why the Romans might have behaved in this way. On the right-hand slab a pig, bull and sheep are being sacrificed in a ceremony which usually marked the beginning of a Roman campaign. Perhaps this was to mark the beginning of the wall at its easterly end.

Shortly afterwards the Romans left Scotland once more and retired to Hadrian's Wall. Roman troops were needed on the Continent again. But the Romans still continued to send scouting parties, and even detachments from the the legions, north of Hadrian's Wall from time to time.

The Last Roman Invasion

In 208 the Emperor Serverus led another Roman army against the Caledonians. A Roman historian wrote:

Severus attacked Caledonia and in making his way through it encountered unspeakable difficulties, cutting down forests, filling in marshes and bridging rivers.

Severus seems to have wanted to occupy Southern Scotland. He led his army as far as Montrose or Stonehaven, but there was no attempt to reoccupy the Antonine Wall. A new fort was built at Carpow and the harbour-fort at Cramond was reoccupied. In 211 Severus's son, Caracalla, ordered a withdrawal to Hadrian's Wall again. The campaign of Severus seems to have been successful for there was peace on the frontier for nearly 100 years. This peace might have been due to the friendship of the Votadini, a large, powerful tribe whose lands lay between the Forth and the Humber—the Romans may have helped the Votadini when they needed it. But Roman scouting parties still searched north of the Antonine Wall. Each year as these scouts passed the wall they must have noticed it was gradually crumbling until finally only memories remained of what it had been. Centuries later the people regarded the remains with much awe because they thought only the Devil could have built such a huge wall. They then called it 'Grim's-dyke' or the 'Devil's Wall'.

In 367 the Caledonians and a tribe from Northern Ireland called the Scots attacked Hadrian's Wall and did much damage. As a Roman historian called Ammian wrote:

> a barbarian alliance brought Britain to her knees.... The Picts plundered at will ... and the Scots.... The Franks raided the Gallic coast [south-east of England] breaking in where they could.

Notice his name for the Caledonians, 'the Picts'.

Although the damage was repaired it was badly done and historians think this was because the Romans were not as careful as they had once been. Less than fifty years later the Roman Legions left Britain for ever. As all over Britain, the different Celtic tribes took over their own defence against the Scots from Ireland, the Picts from the north and the Angles and Saxons from Western Europe. Between the walls the Welsh-speaking Britons of Strathclyde held the south-west of Scotland and their cousins, the Votadini—or Goddodin as they now called themselves—were settled in the south-east. Within a few years the Romans were forgotten.

Life on the Antonine Wall

Soldiers

From the evidence they left we know how the soldiers lived on the Antonine Wall. This wall was never built with the intention of stopping an attack by a large army of several thousand warriors. It was intended to prevent large raiding parties of perhaps 200 to 300 men from getting through or from getting back safely with their loot. Sixteen forts have been found and there were probably another three. The forts provided look-out stations, but there was no rampart on the wall and the soldiers marched along a road behind it.

Legionary soldiers built the wall, for they were architects and masons and carpenters as well as soldiers. They did not guard the wall for they were too valuable to be used for guard duty. The wall was manned by auxiliary soldiers and cavalry units from all over the Empire, with a detachment of Tungrians from modern Belgium at Castlecary and Syrian archers stationed at Bar Hill. After a while new recruits would be drawn from the local area. In this way a soldier of a unit originally from Northern Greece might actually be from Northern England.

In the bigger forts like Cramond there were offices, granaries and blacksmiths' shops as well as barracks for the soldiers. Many of the forts had bath houses which were used as meeting places as much as for keeping clean. Altar stones have been found dedicated to Roman gods such as Jupiter, but the soldiers also seem to have tried to keep the favour of the local gods—at Castlehill an altar has been found dedicated to Britannia.

Civilians

Other people as well as soldiers lived near the wall, especially near the bigger forts. At a dig at Bar Hill in 1902–5 archaeologists discovered a shoe-dump where someone had flung all the old shoes from a cobbler's shop! Although there were many soldiers' shoes, there were also women's and children's. Then in 1956, a stone with an exciting inscription was found at Carriden. Some parts had been worn away, but the letters were clear enough to read. This is a brief translation:

> This stone is dedicated to the god Jupiter by Aelius Mansuestus, who is the representative of the civilian population of Carriden.

A settlement of civilians near a fort, a 'vicus', was made up of ex-soldiers, shopkeepers and traders with their families. When an auxiliary retired at the end of 25 years service he was given Roman citizenship and often married a native woman. Shops were usually set up with their short ends to the street; they would sell wine and salt to the soldiers and the natives would bring their wares to these small markets. In return the traders would bring in goods like pottery, wine and luxury items from all parts of the Empire. These civilian settlements were not deserted when the Romans left the Antonine Wall. For many, life went on as usual after the soldiers had gone, even if they did not have the same number of customers. In Cramond, pottery was found dating from the fourth century AD which shows that the site was still occupied long after the Romans had left.

What the Romans Left

Despite all the fighting and marching and building of forts the Romans do not appear to have left a great deal of evidence. No doubt there is still much to be discovered but, despite all their efforts, the Romans left little impression on Scotland. Perhaps, however, the greatest thing they left behind them cannot be seen or measured, for it was in their time that the first signs of Christianity appeared.

The Carriden Stone

Light on the Dark Ages

The two centuries which follow the collapse of the Roman Empire in the west in the fifth century are sometimes called the 'Dark Ages'. This is because historians have found so little evidence to shed light on how people lived during these years in Europe. If anything, the Dark Ages seem gloomier in Scotland. Lots of important events were happening but we only get tiny glimpses of them through archaeology or the brief jottings of some monk. Sometimes all we have is merely a confusing list of kings, when they reigned and when they were murdered or killed in battle. Even when we find two pieces of evidence about the same event they often contradict each other. To find out about this period of Scottish history we must examine every scrap of evidence we can. We must use chronicles written by monks, archaeological evidence, place names and carvings. Only in this way will we be able to discover more about how the peoples of Scotland lived.

Scots and Picts

Two of the peoples who inhabited Scotland at this time are mentioned by a monk called Gildas. (He lived from c.490–c.570 and was supposed to have been a son of a King of the Britons of Strathclyde.) In about 540 he wrote:

> As the Romans made to go home, there emerged from the coracles that had carried them across the sea valleys [sea lochs], the foul hordes of Scots and Picts like dark throngs of worms. . . . They were to some extent different in their customs but were in perfect accord [agreed] in their greed for bloodshed. . . .

It is quite clear what Gildas thought of the Scots and Picts whom he regarded as barbaric heathens. Gildas was not writing a history but a warning to all the Romano-British rulers to combine before they were swept away by these and other barbarians—the Angles and Saxons from the Continent.

The Picts

Gildas said that the Picts and Scots differed in their customs. Who the Picts were and how they were different from the other peoples who lived in Scotland has caused many quarrels among historians up to the present. An old chronicle written before 995 called the *Chronicle of the Picts* says:

> Cruidne, Cinge's son, the father of the Picts that dwell in this island . . . had seven sons. These are their names: Fib, Fidach, Floclaid, Fortrenn, Cait, Ce, Circinn.

Most historians agree that these are not names of people but of districts occupied by Pictish tribes. 'Fib', they say is Fife; 'Circinn' is Angus and Kincardineshire; 'Fortrenn' lay to the south-west of the River Tay; 'Flocaid' or 'Ath Folta' means Atholl. 'Cait', 'Ce' and 'Fidach' are thought to have lain to the north of the Mounth, and Caithness comes from 'Cait'. The map on the page opposite shows you where historians think the different tribes lived.

Pictish Language

The Picts were the descendants of the fierce Caledonians who fought the Romans. Historians and linguists do not understand their language but some think that it was a mixture of Welsh Celtic and a much older language which was spoken before the Celts arrived. Unfortunately, most examples of Pictish are from gravestones and are very short.

Pictish Customs

The Picts seem to have had one custom which shocked the other races who lived in Scotland—the royal family traced its descent through the mother and not the father. This is how Bede, a monk who lived from c.673–735, tried to explain this Pictish custom. The Picts had settled in Scotland but:

> Having no women with them, these Picts asked wives of the Scots, who consented on condition that, when any dispute arose, they should choose a king from the female royal line rather than the male. This custom continues among the Picts to this day.

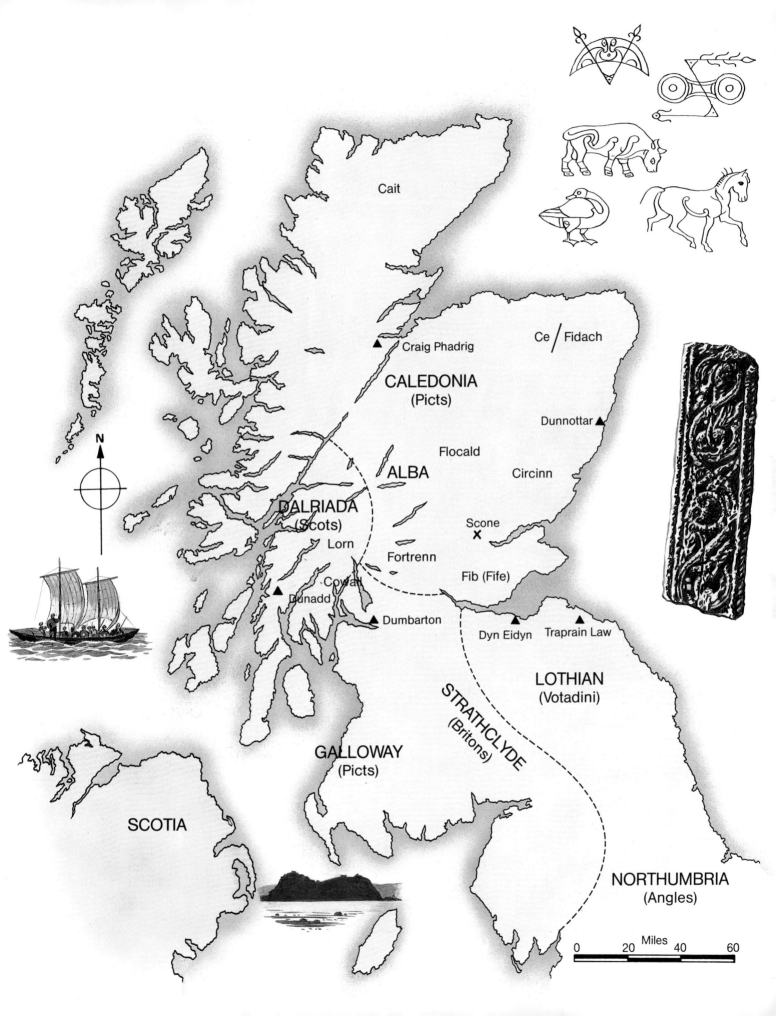

Cait

Craig Phadrig

CALEDONIA
(Picts)

Ce / Fidach

Dunnottar

Flocald

ALBA

Circinn

DALRIADA
(Scots)

Lorn

Scone
✕

Fortrenn

Fib (Fife)

Cowal
Dunadd

Dumbarton

Dyn Eidyn

Traprain Law

LOTHIAN
(Votadini)

STRATHCLYDE
(Britons)

GALLOWAY
(Picts)

SCOTIA

NORTHUMBRIA
(Angles)

N

0   20   Miles   40   60

The daughter of a Pictish king usually married a man from a neighbouring British, Scottish or Northumbrian royal family rather than a Pictish Prince.

This custom is called exogamy (marriage to an outsider). No one is quite sure why the Picts followed this custom but they seem to have been the only people in Western Europe to do it.

A King of the Scots had now become King of the Picts and Scots. It was said that Kenneth McAlpin's mother had been a Pictish Princess. But it is more likely he became King of Scots and Picts because he led a more powerful warband.

Pictish Stones

If you already think the Picts were mysterious, the mystery deepens when we look at the carved standing stones they left. These carvings have been found mainly on the eastern side of the country, from the Northern Isles to the Forth. Some of the stones have crosses on them and are thought to be Christian. The two stones shown on this page will give you an idea of the beauty and liveliness of Pictish carvings.

Perhaps you recognise the strange figure standing in the midst of animals on the stone below from Meigle—Cernunnos, the Lord of the Beasts. The other stone, from Aberlemno Churchyard, shows everyday scenes from Pictish life. Notice the kind of clothes the standing warriors are wearing.

Pictish Mysteries

If you look closely at the top of the Aberlemno stone you will see some unusual carvings. Several Pictish stones bear these strange symbols and many others. Scholars disagree about their meaning; some say they mark the boundaries between two tribes; others maintain they are a record in stone of a marriage treaty. Whatever these symbols did mean is still a mystery—just one more unsolved one surrounding the Picts. Finally, even their disappearance from history is a mystery. In 843 the *Chronicle of the Kings of Scotland* states:

> Kenneth, Alpin's son, reigned over the Scots for sixteen years, after destroying the Picts.

The Britons

To the south of the Forth and Clyde lived the Welsh-speaking Britons. About the year 600 a band of Gododdin warriors, who were the descendants of the Votadini, had their chief oppida at Traprain Law and Dyn Eidyn (probably Edinburgh). The capital of the Kings of Strathclyde was Dumbarton, on the north bank of the Clyde, the 'Dun' or 'Fort of the Britons'. The Britons of Strathclyde are sometimes called the 'Cumbrians'.

About the year 600 a band of warriors from Dyn Eidyn went to fight against the Angles at Catterick in Yorkshire. An old poem, perhaps the oldest Scottish poem, says how the brave 300 went to battle:

> After the wine-feast and the mead-feast they went from us, the mail-clad warriors; I know the grief of their death. Their slaying came to pass before they could grow grey-haired, their host was high-spirited before Catterick—but for one man out of three hundred, none came back.

About 640 the Angles captured Dyn Eidyn and the 'Lallan' or 'Anglish' tongue became the language of the south-east. To the west, the Kingdom of Strathclyde remained independent until about 1018 when Duncan I became King of the Cumbrians (Strathclyde). In 1040 Duncan made his last appearance in Scottish history when he was killed by Macbeth.

The Britons have left traces of where they settled in place names. Names of places beginning with 'aber-' (river mouth) are Welsh-Cumbric. Cramond is the 'Fort (Caer) on the River Almond'. Lanark gets its name from the Cumbric 'lanerc', a 'clear space'. Places like Tranent, Tralorg and Terregles all come from the Cumbric 'tref' meaning a village.

The Angles of Northumbria

You will remember that the Gododdin died at Catterick fighting the heathen Angles of Northumbria. The pagan burials of the Angles in north-east England and south-east Scotland date from the sixth century. By 638 they were laying siege to Edinburgh. The Angles continued to advance to the north until, in 685, their King Egfrith was killed by the Pictish King Brudei at the battle of Nechtansmere (Dunnichen) in Angus. Three centuries later the Scottish victory at Carham on the Tweed in 1016

brought the Lothians and Berwickshire firmly into the Kingdom of Scotia. As well as their place names, which are found mainly in south-east Scotland, the Anglians gave their 'lallan' (lowland) language to the Scottish people.

The Scots

But why is our land 'Scotland' and not 'Pictland' or 'Cumberland'? This extract is from an old document called *De Situ Albanie* (*The Geography of Scotland*):

> The name Argyle [Dalriada] means the shore of the Scots or the Irish, because all Irish and Scots generally are called Gaels.... Fergus MacErc [Erc's son] was first of the descendants of Conaire to receive the kingdom of Scotland....

Although the date given is 501, emigrants from Dalriada, the Scots' homeland in Antrim in Ireland, had probably been coming before that date to New Dalriada. Their chief fort was Dunadd but any advance to the east and south was blocked by the Picts and Britons. In 843 the Scot, Kenneth MacAlpin, became King of the Picts though he had to fight hard for that crown. By 850 he was described as King of Alba, the old Irish name for Scotland. His descendants were crowned at Scone, the old Pictish capital. As you have seen, the Kingdom of Scotia stretched from the Tweed to the Pentland Firth by the eleventh century, though the King's power was still weak in many parts of Scotia.

During these five hundred years the Scots, Britons, Picts and Northumbrians had been brought together into one Kingdom. (A fifth people from the North still remained apart. These were the descendants of the Northmen you will read about in Chapter 5.) The welding together was not only achieved by war. Peace played its part, for the foundations of the nation were not laid until all the different peoples had become Christians.

Celtic Christianity

Christianity had come to Britain while it was still under Roman rule, but the Anglo-Saxon invasion cut off the British Christians from the Roman Christians on the Continent. Gradually these British, or Celtic, Christians began to organise their own Celtic Church.

St Ninian

Bede wrote of the year 565:

> The southern Picts who live this side of the mountains [the Mounth], are said to have abandoned the errors of idolatry [stopped being heathens] long before this date and accepted the true Faith through the preaching of Bishop Ninian, a most reverend and holy man of the British race . . . [whose Church] is known as Candida Casa, the White House, because he built a church of stone, which was unusual among the Britons.

Stone churches might have been unusual among the Britons but Christianity was not. Ninian was not the first Bishop of Whithorn and archaeologists have discovered Christian burials from the fifth century.

St Kentigern

One young man who came to Candida Casa was Kentigern, whose mother was supposed to have been a princess at Traprain Law, one of the oppida of the Gododdin. Kentigern preached among the Southern Picts and later set up his hermit's cell on the banks of the Molendinar River about 600. He was probably the first Bishop of Glasgow. Liek many other early Celtic Christians, Kentigern changed his name when he became a monk and so he is probably better known as St Mungo, the patron saint of Glasgow.

St Patrick

Another saint who came from the Britons of southern Scotland was Patrick. He was born at Dumbarton about 400 and is supposed to have begun his missionary work in Ireland about 432. This was after having been kidnapped by Scottish pirates from that country. He converted many of the Scottish-Irish chiefs and set up a system of churches ruled by bishops. Like all these Celtic saints, Patrick gained a reputation as a magician and is supposed to have rid Ireland of snakes! In his way Patrick was creating an image for the Celtic saints of having magical powers, of being utterly fearless in protecting Christians against pagans and, above all, of trusting utterly in God. Patrick wrote in one hymn:

> Today I arise
> With God my Steersman, stay and guide,
> To guard, to counsel, to hear, to bide
> His way before, His way beside.

Although he became patron saint of Ireland, the bishoprics he created soon gave place to the monasteries which were to be the usual set-up of the Celtic Church.

St Columba

You will read more in the next case history about St Columba, the man, and why he came to convert the Picts. We know that when he landed in Iona in 563 the Southern Picts had already heard Christ's message from Kentigern and other missionaries. But we have learnt more about Columba than any other Celtic saint because his biography or life-story, based on oral evidence, was written by Adomnan, who was Abbot of Iona about 100 years later.

Columba believed that the best way to convert a people was to start with the King and his chief men. That is why he went to King Bridei's capital near Inverness. Adomnan tells of the magic wars between Columba and Bridei's chief druid, Broichan, and of the miracles Columba worked, such as when Columba found the gates of Bridei's fortress bolted against him and magically caused them to be unbolted:

> the king and his council were much afraid . . . and went to meet the holy man with reverence . . . and thenceforth from that day all the days of his life the same ruler honoured the holy and venerable man. . . .

But Columba does not seem to have converted Bridei and his followers, for Adomnan would have been sure to have mentioned this. In fact, it seems that Columba's followers had more success in converting the Picts than the Saint had himself.

Northumbrian Christianity

Iona became the chief missionary centre of Celtic Christianity. Among its many visitors were two young Northumbrian princes, Oswiu and Oswald, who sought shelter there. When Prince Oswald became King of Northumbria he asked the Abbot to send a missionary to spread Christ's word among his people. In 635 the missionary, Aidan, built a monastery on 'Holy Isle' off the coast of Northumbria. Aidan despised riches and once gave Oswald's gift of a fine horse to a beggar, much to the King's annoyance. It was said that when Aidan died a shepherd boy in Tweeddale saw the saint's soul being carried by angels to heaven. The shepherd's name was Cuthbert, who later became the patron saint of the Lothians.

The Venerable Bede

Many of the stories about these Celtic saints were written by Bede, a monk at Jarrow, who died in 735. Bede's main interest was the History of the Church in England. He was very careful in checking his sources of evidence:

> as the laws of history demand, I have laboured honestly to transmit whatever I could learn from common report [what is generally said] for the instruction of posterity [future generations].

The Synod of Whitby

For many years the Celtic and Roman Churches had been separated. In 957, the year that Columba died, Pope Gregory sent St Augustine to set up a mission in Canterbury. From there the Roman Church spread throughout England until it met the Celtic Church in Northumbria.

Owing to their separation the two Churches celebrated Easter on different dates. This was a matter of great concern as the followers of one Church would be rejoicing that Christ had risen while those in the other Church would still be mourning his death. This especially troubled King Oswiu who followed the Celtic Church's date while his newly-wedded wife was a Roman Christian.

In 664 representatives of the two churches met at Whitby in Yorkshire. After much debate King Oswiu said he would choose the Roman dating. He said that since Jesus had given the keys of Heaven to St Peter, the first Bishop of Rome, he might deny Oswiu entry into Heaven for choosing the wrong date for Easter! In fact, Oswiu had probably made up his mind already to choose the Roman Church in order to keep Northumbria with the rest of England and the Continental churches.

The Celtic Church

In the Celtic Church the Abbot of a monastery was often more important than the Bishop in whose see or district the monastery lay. The monastery was the main centre of religious activity in the Celtic Church, another important difference from the Roman Church. Also, in a Celtic monastery like Iona, each monk had his own beehive-shaped cell, and the monks did not live together in the way that the Roman Benedictine monks lived. Celtic monks would also go out and teach and preach to the people, unlike the Benedictines who always stayed in their monastery.

Beehive cells

You must not imagine that all these Celtic saints or monks had to do was travel into heathen lands for the people there immediately to become Christians. It was always dangerous and often fatal to try and convert the pagan Celts. The warriors and druids resented Christian missionaries who wanted to overthrow pagan Celtic customs. The warriors and druids were the most respected people in Celtic life and they disliked missionaries who preached that everyone was equal in the sight of the Christian God. The warrior-class did not take to a God of Peace and Love who had chosen to sacrifice Himself. They probably never understood the idea of a meek and merciful God. But to the ordinary people the Celtic missionaries brought hope of everlasting life to everyone; not just to warriors who could feast and fight for evermore. Celtic missionaries travelled all over Europe, to Germany and even to Russia. Their monasteries became places of study for they were among the foremost teachers of their day and did much to keep learning alive during the Dark Ages. In Scotland, however, they did more than this: the Celtic Church helped to weld together in a common faith the different peoples who lived there.

Something to Remember

This chapter has been about an important and confusing period in the history of the Scottish people. Four of the five peoples who were going to make up the Scottish nation appeared between 400 and 600. These were the Picts, Britons, Angles and Scots. The homeland of the Picts seems to have been on the eastern side of the country between the Forth and the Moray Firth. The Britons lived mainly in the lands between the two Roman walls and spoke a language which was the ancestor of modern Welsh. The Angles of Northumbria had occupied the lands between the Forth and the Tweed and south to the Humber. The Scots were Goidelic-speaking Celts from north-east Ireland who, starting in Dalriada, eventually gave their name to the whole country ruled by the descendants of Kenneth MacAlpin.

This unity was largely brought about by the missionaries of the Celtic Church. They were holy men who converted the pagan Scots, Picts and Northumbrians. The missionaries brought with them a new faith and a new hope. For their faith they were prepared to endure great hardships and suffering. They also brought with them a joy in learning, and their monasteries were centres of light in dark times.

Something to Think About

Like most other nations in the world today, the Scots are not thoroughbreds with 'pure' blood in their veins. You have seen how, even at an early stage, there were at least four different peoples living in Scotland and that most of us are living mixtures of these peoples.

In this confusing period of Scottish history we have seen how different kinds of evidence have been used to build up some picture of what was happening at that time. Archaeology has proved useful in showing differences in customs and cultures, but it can only tell us a limited amount. We can quote primary written sources but although they are very valuable we must not rely on them too much. We must be like Bede and find as many sources as we can and then be careful how we use them. Place names can tell us more but they, too, can prove unreliable. Pictish symbol stones tell us much about the customs and costumes of the time, but we must beware of putting our ideas into the minds of people in the past.

The Two Columbas

Adomnan, Abbot of Iona, wrote the *Life of Columba* nearly one hundred years after the saint's death in 597. He was not writing a full biography of Columba when he collected all the information he could about the saint. He wanted only to show how holy a man Columba had been. All writers of saints' lives did this in Adomnan's time. It was believed that the holier the saint, the more miracles he performed, and so Adomnan tells us in detail about Columba's miracles such as the time when the saint protected one of his followers from a savage water beast in Loch Ness.

But Adomnan's *Life* is not just a collection of wild stories about a famous old holy man. It tells us much about what was happening in Scotland and Ireland at that time, how people lived and what they thought. Above all, it tells us what kind of a person Columba was in real life. But we must be careful here for he wants to protect the character of his hero. We must, as it were, read between the lines and watch carefully for the things that Adomnan says very little about or glosses over quickly.

Near the beginning of his *Life* Adomnan has this to say of Columba:

> For he was angelic in appearance, polished in speech, holy in work, excellent in intelligence, great in resourcefulness.... He could not pass even the interval of one hour without setting himself either to prayer, or to reading, writing, or even to some [manual] labour.

This is an excellent character reference well befitting a saint.

Before this Adomnan tells us:

> In the second year after the battle of Cuil-dremne, in the forty-second year of his life, he [Columba] sailed over from Ireland to Britain, wishing to live in pilgrimage for Christ's sake.

To go on a pilgrimage and convert pagans to Christianity would add even more to the holiness of the saintly man. But why mention a battle? Is there any connection between the two events?

Columba is Excommunicated

Of some events which took place in the year 561 Adomnan has this to say:

> When St Columba was being excommunicated by a certain synod [church meeting] for some venial [pardonable] and indeed excusable sins, unjustly, as afterwards became plain in the end, he came to the same assembly that had collected against himself.

Excommunication meant the cutting off of some sinner from the church and from its services. If this was a punishment bad enough for any ordinary person, imagine how much greater must it have been for someone like Columba! Excommunication was a very serious affair and was not passed on someone whose sins were light, certainly not for 'venial and indeed excusable sins'. This meeting of churchmen must have had some very good reason for even thinking about excommunicating Columba. But Adomnan passes over the matter quickly and tells us of a vision by Brendan which forbade anyone to harm Columba. Adomnan does not tell us why the synod was called, nor does he tells us what sins Columba was accused of committing.

The battle of Cuil-dremne metioned by Adomnan may give us an answer to the mystery. Two old Irish chronicles tell of Columba's part in this battle. *The Chronicle of Tigernach* says:

> The battle of Cuil-dremne [was won] over [King] Diarmait ... through the prayers of Columcille [Columba], who said, 'O God, why clearest thou not away the mist, that we might reckon the number of the host that reaps judgments off us [that fights us]. A host marching round a cairn, the son of storm [the wind] betrays them; [because] my wizard, who will not deny me, is God's son [Jesus], who will assist me.'

The question was, should a holy man take part in a battle, as this chronicle seems to suggest Columba did and, worse still, should he use magic, even God's magic, to kill men? Columba was indeed blamed for the death of many men and he was also blamed for having caused the battle in the first place. It was said that Diarmait, Columba's own kinsman, had ordered the killing of an Irish prince who was under the Saint's protection. Also, Diarmait had ordered Columba to return to its original owner a copy of a book which Columba had written himself. Worst of all, Columba had persuaded his other kinsmen to fight against King Diarmait.

Another old Irish chronicle from this time mentions that Columba went to Laisran, his priest or confessor, and asked how he could be forgiven for causing so many deaths. Laisran told him to leave Ireland for ever and go to Pictland and there save as many souls as had been killed in the battle of Cuil-dremne. The chronicle says that this was Columba's reason for coming to Scotland. It is possible that the Synod passed this sentence on Columba in return for lifting the excommunication.

Columba's Real Character

What Adomnan had to say about the character of Columba was true. But there were other sides to his character which Adomnan did not mention. Like any Celtic prince, for both his parents were of royal blood, Columba was proud of his descent. A *Homily on St Columba* says:

> Columcille's [Columba's] descent was noble.... He had by descent the right to the kingship of Ireland, and it would have been offered to him had he not renounced it for God....

He was also quick-tempered, at least in the years in Ireland. He was as touchy as any Celtic warrior when his pride was hurt. He was used to getting his own way and was quick to punish anyone who hindered God's work. He was always interested in warriors' work and may even have borne the scars from an old battle wound.

So we have another side of Columba's character to put alongside Adomnan's. But we must not condemn Adomnan for suppressing the truth. He wanted to write about a good man who had carried out God's work with passion and energy. Adomnan was not writing a 'History of St Columba'. If he had been doing so then he should have mentioned the darker sides of Columba's character. As historians, however, we have a duty to look at all the evidence, whether good or bad, and even to look between the lines for the things that are not written.

The Coming of the Northmen

Scattered Finds

Look at the pictures on this page. They are of finds from different parts of the world. Though the stone lion sits in Venice it originally came from Piraeus near Athens in Greece. On the lion's left shoulder a message has been carved. The letters are runes, the Viking alphabet. The little statue of Buddha, which must have been made in India or the Far East, was found in Sweden. The skeletons of the man, woman and children are from a Viking grave in Western Greenland. The wooden posts with the intertwining branches were uncovered by archaeologists in Dublin and once formed part of the wall of a Viking house.

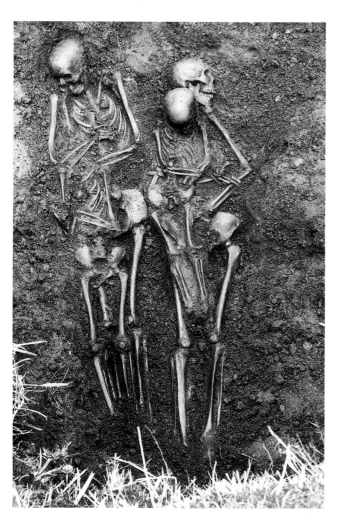

Exporting People

There is a common link between all these scattered finds. They are all connected with the travels and settlements of the Vikings.

Someone once said that Scotland's greatest export was its people and the same can be said about the Vikings. Between the ninth and twelfth centuries thousands of people left Denmark, Norway and Sweden to seek a new life in other countries. Today, many people leave or emigrate from their home countries in search of a new life. Sometimes they do this because they cannot make a good living in their own homelands, sometimes because another country sounds so attractive. Most people emigrate for a mixture of reasons. Perhaps you can think of some.

If you look at a map of Norway you can see that there are many mountains and hundreds of sea-lochs or fiords. This is how Adam of Bremen, who came from north Germany, described the land of the Northmen in 1070:

> The soil in Jutland [Denmark] is sterile [will not grow crops]; except for places near a river, nearly everything looks like a desert. Norway is the most barren of all countries because of its rugged mountains and extreme cold. But part of Sweden is fertile, the land is rich in fruit and honey.

This diagram and the one opposite show the effects of overpopulation in Scandinavia.

Where the Vikings voyaged

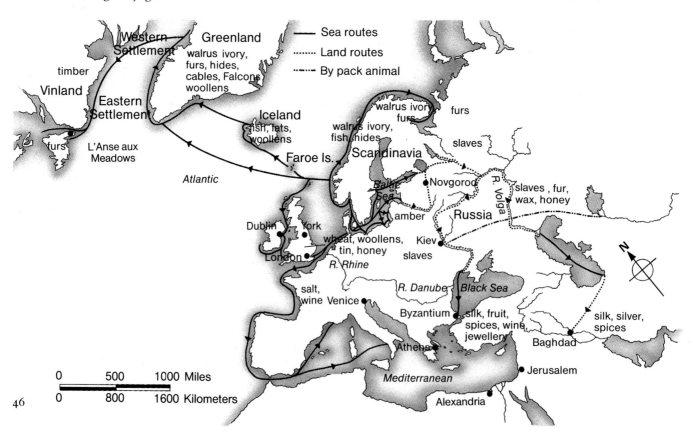

carnage [slaughter] and captivity. Some of the monasteries and other places near the [River] Seine they devastated [destroyed] and the rest they filled with terror, having received much money.

Think why the Vikings might have liked to attack monasteries, and notice what other kind of booty the Vikings acquired according to the French monk.

There was also this sinister entry in *The Annals of Ulster* for the year 806:

The community of Iona was slain by the gentiles [heathen Northmen], that is to say sixty-eight [monks].

This poem was spoken by a young Viking:

My mother once told me
She'd buy me a longship
A handsome vessel
To go sailing with the Vikings
To stand at the sternpost
And steer a fine warship
Then head back for harbour
And hew down some foemen.

Ships and Sailors

The Northmen were skilful seamen who built fine ships which did not need to keep to very deep water. In this way the Vikings were able to sail up rivers and creeks and attack inland towns and villages far away from the sea. The word 'Viking' probably comes from an old Norse word meaning 'the men from the viks or creeks'.

Dragon Ships

The Northmen built two kinds of ships; the longship for raiding and the 'knorr' for trading. The young Viking wanted a longship or 'drakkar' whose bows were shaped like huge snakes or dragons which gave these ships their name. On p 48 you can see a picture of a Viking drakkar which archaeologists found near Gokstad in south-west Norway in 1881.

The Gokstad ship is 76 feet (23m) long and 17 feet (5m) wide, and you can see that it was called a longship from its long and narrow shape. It could sail or be rowed in water as shallow as 33″ (0.85m), and when it was fully laden there was only about a metre of the ship's side above the water-line. As they aproached some defenceless village the drakkars must

As you can see, crops would be difficult to grow in most parts of Scandinavia where the Northmen or Vikings came from. Imagine what would happen if the number of people increased and it became more and more difficult to feed them.

Fishers, Traders and Raiders

Some Northmen became fishermen and then discovered that they could grow richer by trading than by fishing. When they were not trading their goods, some traders found it profitable to become pirates and raiders. So it was often difficult to tell when the Northmen were peaceable merchants and when they were fierce pirates. Soon the Northmen moved on from pirating ships to raiding on land, and these Viking raiders gained a terrible reputation all over Western Europe. In 841 a French monk wrote of what happened to the people of Rouen in northwest France when the Northmen raided it:

fire and sword, they [the Vikings] gave up the city, the monks and the rest of the people to have seemed like menacing sea-creatures to the terrified villagers.

Without the longships there would have been no Vikings. Ships and warriors were like the Vikings' favourite weapon—the battle-axe. The longships were the handle of the battle-axe which delivered the blow of the blade—the Viking warriors. One was useless without the other. But with each ship carrying from 40 to 50 fighting men the Vikings were able to launch devastating raids without warning on the coasts of their victims. Naturally, the Vikings were proud of their longships and a Viking chief would have his new ship decorated by the best wood carvers he could find. The Vikings gave their ships strange and beautiful names such as *Dragon Head*, and *Long Serpent*.

In 1893 some Norwegians set out to prove that a longship could sail long distances across the stormiest seas. In that year they built an exact copy of the Gokstad ship right down to the tiniest detail. On 30 April a crew set sail across the Atlantic and reached Newfoundland 27 days later. In spite of some rough weather the crew was never in any great danger from the ship sinking. The voyage was a tribute to the skills of the old and new Norse shipbuilders, and to the courage and seamanship of the ancient and modern Vikings.

Knorrs

The other main type of ship used by the Northmen, the 'knorrs' or 'knarrs', were not used to carry warriors, but merchants' goods and settlers seeking new homes. The knorr was about the same length as a longship, but wider and lying deeper in the water. There was often a deck over part of the ship to keep cargo and crew dry. Knorrs mainly travelled under sail, though oars were used getting in and out of harbour.

The Northmen Go West

In their longships and knorrs the Northmen journeyed to the places you read about at the beginning of this chapter. We know a great deal about these voyages from the 'sagas' or stories that the Viking poets wrote. The sagas also describe the dangers they faced during their voyages and the life they led when they settled down in their new homelands.

A drakkar

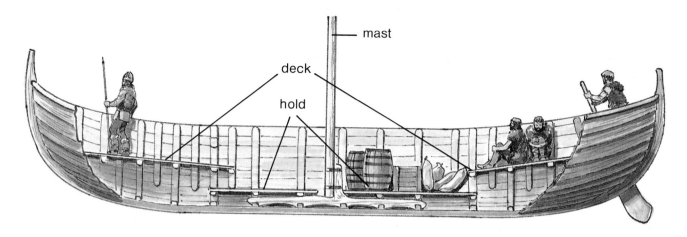

Section through a knorr

Orkney and Shetland

The sagas tell us that these islands were first settled by the Northmen who were driven out of Norway by King Harald Harfrage [Fair-hair], and then:

> One summer Harald went to the West across the sea to punish the Vikings as he was weary of their devastations ... Harald subdued Shetland, the Orkneys and Hebrides. ...

If these Vikings wanted to escape King Harald's wrath they would surely have to go further west.

Iceland

Most sagas say they went to Iceland. But another saga, written about 860, tells a different story about the settlement of Iceland. In this saga the Vikings discovered:

> The land Iceland ... Floki gave the land a bad name, Herjolf had good and bad to say of it, while Thorolf swore that butter dripped from every blade of grass in the land they had found, and for that reason he was nicknamed Thorolf Butter.

Think which of these sagas is likely to be nearest the truth. Remember that Iceland did not mean 'a land of ice' to the Vikings, it was just their word for 'island'.

Further Westwards

Imagine the North Atlantic to be a wide river and the islands in it like stepping-stones. We have already seen three of the stones, Shetland, Orkney and Iceland, and a saga describes how the Vikings reached the next one. It tells how a fierce, troublesome Viking called Erik the Red was ordered to leave Iceland for he had caused the death of several men by his

fighting and quarrelling. He was told not to return until three years had passed. Erik was not a man to waste his time so he decided to voyage to the west to see if fishermen's tales of a great island there were true. After many days' sailing, Erik found a land which he christened 'Greenland' because, as he said, that name would make people want to come and settle there.

Erik was right for many settlers came, and now, says the story teller:

> The farmers there raise many cattle and sheep, they live mainly on these foods and beef and they also eat caribou, whale, seals and bears.

The climate of Greenland today is harsh, so you may be surprised to learn that these early settlers also grew corn. Some historians think that at that time the climate was much milder than it is today. This may also be the reason why the Vikings were able to make such long voyages.

Vinland the Good

The photograph at the bottom of p 52 shows a reconstruction of a Viking long-house. This was made by Canadian archaeologists near the ruins where Vikings settled in Newfoundland. It is possible that the Vikings sailed south along the North American coast as far as New England. The sagas tell how Leif Eriksson, son of Erik the Red, discovered a land so fertile that even vines grew wild there and they called this land Vinland the Good. Though the land was rich the Vikings did not settle there for long because they were attacked by the 'skraelings', the Viking name for Indians. Near Leif's first settlement archaeologists found traces of a smithy with a few pieces of smelted bog-iron. A Carbon-14 dating of these pieces of iron gave a date of 1070±70 years, about the time when the Vikings were exploring that part of America. Now, the Indians at that time did not know how to smelt and shape iron. In fact they did not learn how to do so until Europeans taught them in the sixteenth century. Put these pieces of evidence together and see what conclusions you come to.

The Last Vikings

The Viking settlements in Greenland lasted until nearly the end of the fifteenth century. Then the weather seems to have grown much colder and another group of hostile 'skraelings', the Eskimoes, attacked the Vikings. It is strange to think that the last Viking settlers in Greenland were dying off just at the same time as Columbus was making his voyages to the Americas.

Eastwarding

The Vikings who sailed across the Atlantic and settled on the islands there came mostly from Norway. Another group, mostly from Sweden, went eastwards. These Vikings were traders rather than raiders or settlers. They sailed across the Baltic Sea and up the River Dvina which took them deep into the heart of what is now the U.S.S.R. When they reached the head-waters of the Dvina, the Vikings either took their ships to pieces or dragged them and their cargoes to the head waters of another great river which flowed eastward. Along the banks of these rivers they built trading stations like Novgorod and Kiev, which became the first Russian towns. In fact, the modern Russian word 'gorod'—a town—comes from the Norse 'garth', a fenced enclosure. The Northmen traded the furs they got from the Russian tribes for the luxury goods of the Mediterranean in the markets of 'Miklagarth'—'The Huge City'—which was their name for Constantinople.

How Others Saw the Northmen

Early in the tenth century an Arab traveller called Ibn Rustab met some Vikings in Russia. He described them like this:

> They have no domains [lands], settlements or fields; their only business is to trade in sable and squirrel skins and other kinds of skins.... In payment they take coins, which they keep in their belts.

Perhaps some Viking trader took a fancy to the little statue of the Buddha which he took home with him to Sweden when his trading days were over.

Another Arab, Ibn Fadlan, travelled all the way from Baghdad in Iraq to the River Volga. He said the Northmen were very handsome in appearance and as tall as date palms but were very dirty!

The Gods of the Northmen

Another scene that Ibn Fadlan saw was the funeral of a Viking chief which ended with the bodies of the chief and a slave-woman being burnt in a ship. A Viking turned to Ibn Fadlan and said:

> We ... burn them in an instant, so that they go to Paradise in that very hour.

You have probably heard of the Up Helly—a ceremony which still takes place in Shetland today, when models of a Viking chief and his ship are burned.

Odin

The Viking was sure that his chief was going to join Odin, the greatest god in Valhalla, the warriors' Paradise.

A nineteenth-century artist's impression of Odin. Notice the ravens on his shoulder.

Odin is the highest and oldest of the gods. He governs all things and however mighty the other gods might be, they all obey him as children do their father.

That was how an Icelandic poet described Odin, the god of battle whose magic spear would decide which side would win. He was also the god of wisdom, because he had sacrificed an eye for a drink from the fountain of wisdom. This is why Odin was sometimes called 'The One-Eyed'. Another of his names was 'All-Knowing' for he had two ravens, Mind and Memory, which brought him all the news of what was going on in the world each day.

He was also known as 'The Lord of the Gallows' because his magic made hanged men tell him all their secrets. Some Swedish tribes would even hang men in Odin's honour. In 1950 several bodies were found in a peat-bog in Tollund in Denmark. One was so well preserved that the archaeologists could even tell what he had eaten for his last meal. He had been strangled before he was buried for there were two leather ropes wrapped tightly around his neck. The archaeologists think the man went willingly to his death for his face was calm. Perhaps the Tollund man was sacrificed to 'The Lord of the Gallows'.

The Lewis chessmen

Odin's name comes from an old Norse word meaning madness or frenzy, and he would fill warriors with his madness until they feared nothing. These mad warriors, called 'berserkers', would grow so impatient to begin a battle that they would bite their shields just like the berserker chessman which was found on the island of Lewis.

The Tollund man

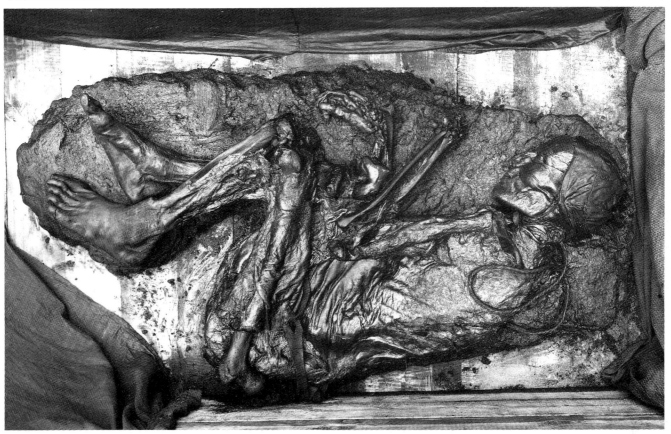

Thor

The Norse poets mentioned Odin so often because he was the god of poetry. But though Odin was feared and respected, the Northmen's favourite god was Thor. He was tall, red–headed and very strong. He was a storm-god; his name means 'Thunder'. As Thor controlled the winds, the Northmen were always very careful to pray to him before setting out on a voyage, even after they became Christians! There is a picture of Thor with his great hammer on this page. Thor's favourite pastime was braining un-friendly giants with his hammer!

Other Gods

The Northmen had many other gods. One of them, Loki, was disliked because he was always stirring up trouble. Loki's daughter, Hel, was so ugly and fear-some that Odin sent her to the Underworld to look after the souls of the dead. You can guess what her kingdom was called! The Anglo-Saxons who in-vaded England in the fifth century also worshipped Thor and Odin, whom they called Woden, as well as other gods, Frey and Tiu. You will notice a connec-tion between these gods and some of the names of the days of the week.

Reconstruction of a Viking long-house at L'Anse aux Meadows, Newfoundland

The Northmen at Home

The long-houses that Leif Eriksson and his men built in Newfoundland (see reconstruction on opposite page) were the kind of houses that Northmen built wherever they went, especially where wood was difficult to find. The remains of a Viking settlement were found at Jarlshof on the southernmost tip of Shetland. From 1949 archaeologists began to uncover a large village which had been occupied by Northmen from the ninth to the sixteenth centuries. The picture above gives you an artist's impression of how the village must have looked in the times of the Northmen.

Notice the materials the Northmen used to build their houses, and the ropes across their roofs. The house in the front centre was built by the earliest settlers. In the picture it is no longer used for human occupation. The way the two long walls at the end of the house are placed will tell you why.

Life at Jarlshof
Here is a list of some of the artefacts which the archaeologists found at Jarlshof: weaving tools, long pins made of bronze and whale bone, combs, stone sinkers for fishing lines, sheep, cattle, pig and pony bones, counters and dice. Archaeologists were able to use these to find out what sort of life the Northmen at Jarlshof lived and to decide whether they were raiders, settlers or traders.

Norse Words Today

The Northmen left other kinds of evidence for us today. Their name for an island was '-ey' or '-ay' and so we have names like Orkney and Colonsay to show where they settled. 'Dale' meant a valley such as Arisdale in Shetland and Ormidale in Arran. Think of their name for a creek and of any place-names today which resemble it. 'By' was the Northmen's name for a farm or a town. Perhaps you can guess what a 'by-law' is. The Northmen gave their names to other things as well. Words like 'egg', 'sky', 'get' and 'gift' are only some of the gift-words from this hardy and adventurous people.

Runes
You will recall the markings on the lion's shoulder in Venice. They are the Northmen's letters called 'runes'. The runic alphabet was called 'Futhark' from the first six letters. At the top of p 54 you will see a photograph of some runes.

Viglakr's rune

Rune-stones have been found wherever the Northmen went. There is one in the Museum of Antiquities in Edinburgh. It has this simple inscription:

Viglakr, the King's Staller [Marshall] cut these runes

They were cut in August or September 1263 just before the Battle of Largs when a great Viking army under King Haakon was defeated by the Scots. This was the last Viking invasion of Scotland.

Something to Remember

The Northmen came to Scotland at the end of the eighth century. They arrived at first as raiders but later settled in such large numbers in some parts of Scotland that they left a permanent mark on the land and people of these parts. This invasion was only a small part of the wanderings of the Northmen which took them to the eastern coast of America and to Constantinople.

They were a tough and adventurous people who endured many hardships voyaging in their longships and knorrs. Sometimes they sought plunder; sometimes they were seeking for new lands to settle. Wherever they went they left a legacy for future peoples. Their gods were warriors and poets, occupations that the Northmen admired.

Something to Think About

We must remember that many of the things which made the Northmen leave their homeland are the same as those which make people emigrate from Scotland today. They wanted a new life and, if possible, a more prosperous one. Many went for adventure and left their bones in graves far from their homeland. Some went as traders, many of them retiring back home as successful merchants.

They left traces wherever they went. Many of our Scottish place-names are those given by the Northmen. In England, Ireland and France, too, they have left a legacy of place-names, such as Normandy, recalling their settlers in these lands.

Although best known as raiders and pirates, for they did cause many deaths and much destruction, the Northmen should not be remembered for this alone. Much more important were the peaceful settlers who came afterwards and settled down whose descendants make up an important part of the Scottish people today.

THE NORTHMEN

700	
800	793 Lindisfarne attacked
	806 Iona sacked
	841 Vikings at Dublin and Rouen
	860 Settlement on Iceland
900	
	922 Ibn Fadlan
	984 Settlement on Greenland
1000	
	1066 Battle of Hastings
1100	1070 Vikings at Vinland

The Queen who was a Saint

Of all the living persons whom I know or have known she was the most devoted to prayer and fasting, to works of mercy and alms-giving [charity].

These words were written about St Margaret by her own priest, Turgot.

Margaret was born in Hungary about 1046, the daughter of an English prince who had been exiled. Her mother was the daughter of King Stephen who later became the patron saint of the Hungarians. Margaret was, therefore, the granddaughter of two kings. When her father died Margaret and her family returned to England in 1066, but soon had to flee because her brother led an uprising against William the Conqueror. They decided to seek shelter with Malcolm III of Scotland. Malcolm 'Canmore' had spent some years at the English court before winning the Scottish crown from King Macbeth.

After a rough voyage the refugees landed at a cove on the Forth which is still called St Margaret's Hope. They had been seen by Malcolm's men, and the King himself arrived and invited them to stay at his 'palace' at Dunfermline. Margaret's family must have been worried by this invitation for they knew that 'Malcolm the Big Chief', as his name means in Gaelic, was a fierce, often cruel, warrior-king.

When they saw Malcolm's palace the weary travellers must have thought they had arrived in a land of barbarians. They were used to the comfortable courts of England and Hungary, and Malcolm's 'palace' was dirty and uncomfortable. It was more like a fort than a king's dwelling place.

It was not long before they received another shock. Malcolm told them he had fallen in love with Margaret and wanted to marry her! Not only had he been married before, but he was twice her age. In any case Margaret did not want to marry anyone for she wished to become a nun. Malcolm was determined however and, as a chronicler of the time wrote:

He [Malcolm] dealt with her brother until he said 'Yea', for in truth he durst [dared] not say otherwise seeing they had come into Malcolm's power.

Margaret finally agreed, and she and Malcolm were married at Dufermline in 1070. Malcolm remained a devoted husband for the rest of his life. They had eight children; two daughters and six sons, three of whom became Kings. Turgot wrote this about Malcolm:

he readily obeyed her wishes and prudent counsels [wise advice] in all things. Whatever she refused, he refused also; whatever pleased her, he also loved for the love of her.

Although Malcolm was the king, notice how he obeyed her wishes.

Although she did not become a nun, Margaret never lost her devotion to the Church. She wanted to bring the Celtic Church nearer to her Roman Church. Malcolm could speak Gaelic and she used him to translate for her when she was talking to Celtic churchmen. Turgot tells us:

To these [Margaret's arguments] they could not answer a word and now knowing the meaning of the [Roman] Church's practices, obeyed them ever after.

Perhaps having the King as her interpreter made the Celtic churchmen more eager to listen to Margaret's arguments!

One change Margaret made is still with us today. She persuaded Malcolm and his nobles, and through them the rest of the Scots, to keep Sunday as a holy day. Before her time, as Turgot said, the people had devoted:

themselves to every kind of worldly business upon it just as they did upon other days.

Margaret invited monks from England to the new Abbey she built in Dunfermline. She also sent monks to restore the Abbey at Iona which the Northmen had destroyed. Turgot tells us that she did much to help the poor. She looked after two dozen poor people all the year round, giving them food, shelter and clothing. Every morning she fed nine orphans with her own spoon, a remarkable thing for a Queen to do! Turgot said the only time she ever became angry was when anyone tried to prevent the poor from coming to her.

Malcolm built a new palace for her on the Rock at Edinburgh. There she had her own little chapel which still stands in the Castle. According to Turgot, Margaret made many improvements to the royal palaces. She had rich cloth brought from abroad for the tables and walls. She made the nobles behave themselves differently when eating at the royal table. Each noble was given his own drinking-cup instead of sharing one with others. She stopped all the brawling and drunkenness that had taken place in the King's palace before she came. Margaret even made the nobles say a short prayer of thanks before they rose from the table at the end of a meal!

Through these changes Margaret encouraged foreign merchants to trade with Scotland. In this way she helped the Scots to come into contact with England and countries on the Continent. This trade also helped the Scots to prosper.

Margaret knew the best way to bring more gentle and civilised manners was to start with Malcolm and her own children. This is how Turgot said she brought up her own children:

> She took all care that they should be well brought up, and especially that they should be trained in virtue [goodness]. . . . She charged [told] the governor who had care of the nursery to curb the children, to scold them, and to whip them whenever they were naughty.

Margaret sincerely believed that more civilised manners and foreign ways would help the Scots. But perhaps she went too far for some of them. None of her sons were given the names of Scottish kings. Later, her sons had much trouble from those Scots who did not like Margaret's 'foreign' ways.

In 1093 Malcolm was killed while leading a raid into England. Margaret had tried to stop him for she feared for his safety. Turgot tells us that on the day he was killed and before any messenger could bring the news of his death, Margaret had said:

> Perhaps on this very day a heavy calamity [disaster] may befall the realm of Scotland as it has not been for many ages past.

A few days later when she was dying from a painful illness, Margaret asked for her Black Cross. This was a beautiful ornamented black box containing a splin-

A fifteenth-century illustration of St Margaret.

ter of wood believed to have come from the Holy Rood or Cross on which Jesus was crucified. Her son Edgar arrived from the battlefield, but did not want to distress his mother and so he told Margaret that Malcolm was well. Margaret begged him to tell her the truth and, finally, he did. She then said a short prayer and died. Years later, Margaret's youngest son, David I, founded a monastery for the safe-keeping of the Holy Rood.

As soon as she was dead people began to call Margaret a saint, but it was not until 1249 that the Church made her one.

In early Scottish history we know more about St Margaret than any other person except Columba. We know so much because Turgot wrote her life story. He was English and was very loyal to her. She had picked him to be her confessor, her own priest. Later on, one of her sons made him Bishop of St Andrews, the chief Bishop in Scotland. Turgot wrote his

Life of St Margaret for her daughter, Matilda, who was Queen of England. Because he was Margaret's confessor he thought he was the best person to write her biography:

> My evidence is especially trustworthy, since . . . I am acquainted with the most part of her secrets.

But we must be aware of the possibility that he might not have been the best person to write about Margaret.

Suppose you wrote a biography of your best friend and only included his or her good points. This would not be very reliable evidence about your friend as even the best of friends have some faults. It is the duty of biographers and historians to reveal their subject's good and bad points.

> Were I tempted to recount [tell] all that I could to her honour, it might be thought that, under cover of your [Matilda's] mother's praises, I was flattering your own queenly dignity. But . . . I add nothing to the truth.

Perhaps Turgot thought that this statement would make his biography seem more reliable, though he still does not contemplate that Margaret had bad points.

Turgot's *Life of St Margaret* shows us one of the great problems facing historians. We must always pay attention to the story of someone who knew a great person or who took part in some event. But we must always be careful how much we can rely on his words if he admired—or disliked—that person. Before making up your mind you must carefully consider what that person wrote or said, and who they were. Think whether they might have something to gain or lose by what they said. Above all, remember to ask yourself who they were writing for.

A 'Devil's advocate' is a person who sets out to find out everything bad about a person like St Margaret who has the reputation of being very good. If you were to write a biography of St Margaret, consider whether you would agree with Turgot or be a 'Devil's advocate'.

6 The Normans Invade Scotland

What's in a Name?

If you ever wondered where Scottish surnames came from, you probably discovered that people whose name is Anderson once had an ancestor who was the son of Andrew, that Watson means 'the son of Walter'. In Gaelic, 'Mac' means 'the son of', so it is obvious what Macdonald means. Some of our names come from the trade or profession of one of our forefathers. 'Baxter' is the old Scottish word for a baker, and those of you who are called Webster had a forefather who was a weaver.

We Scots have also taken our names from other countries. 'Inglis' tells us that one of our ancestors came from England. You can probably guess what countries 'Walsh', 'Wallace' and 'Fleming' came from. Many of our names came from that part of France called Normandy. Perhaps you can recall how Normandy received its name. There are many 'Norman' names in Scotland such as Melville, Sommerville, Montgomery, Cummings, Bruce, Graham and Lindsay. Let us now see why Norman names are so common in Scotland.

The First Normans in Scotland

The first Normans arrived in Scotland during the reign of Malcolm and his Queen, Margaret. But it was their youngest son, David I, who especially welcomed the Normans and encouraged them to settle here. Before he became King of the Scots in 1124 David had spent many years at the court of the Kings of England, where the dynasty or family of William the Conqueror, Duke of Normandy, had reigned since his victory at Hastings in 1066. During his years at the English court, David had picked up many Anglo-Norman ideas and had made many Anglo-Norman friends. The Norman Kings of England also gave lands to David and, as Earl of Huntingdon, he was one of the greatest English lords and had to swear an oath of loyalty to the English Kings.

When he became King, David was faced by the men of Moray rebelling against him and his 'foreign' ways and advisors. To help him defeat the rebels, David received much help from the Anglo-Norman barons who sent to him their younger sons who would not inherit the family titles and estates. It was these younger sons who were the ancestors of some of the greatest families in Scotland.

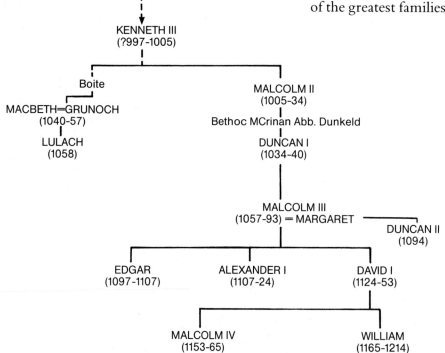

Kings of the Scots, Kenneth McAlpin to William the Lyon

An Oath of Loyalty

David I had to think of a way to encourage these Anglo-Normans to come to Scotland. Although he could give them land, he had to make sure they would remain loyal to him. To do this he borrowed a Norman idea. He made them swear an oath of loyalty to him. It was called 'homage' from the French word 'homme'—a man—and by this oath they became David's men. During the act of homage the baron would place his hands between those of the King and swear the following oath:

> I, Freskin of Strathbrok, swear on these holy gospels of God that from this hour till the last day of my life I shall be faithful to you, my Lord, the King. I swear that I shall never knowingly take part in council, battle, deed or conspiracy [plot] in which you shall lose your life or receive any hurt, injury or insult to your person . . . and I shall never knowingly do anything in my own person to bring harm or insult to you.

The oath of loyalty

You can see that the act of homage was a very solemn occasion. It placed very heavy duties on the baron, so let us see what he got in return.

The agreement between the King and baron was written down on a 'charter' which was signed by both the King and the baron. As most barons did not know how to write in those days they had a seal made which stamped their signature or family crest on wax. The King's secretary or Chancellor kept a copy of the charter and the baron put another copy in his 'Charter chest' for safekeeping. Here is part of a Charter which William the Lyon, the grandson of David I gave to the Scottish-Norman baron, Robert de Brus:

> I regrant [give again] and confirm to Robert de Brus all the lands which his father and he held in Annandale . . . as freely as his father and he held it in the time of King David I . . . for the service of ten knights. . . . I [William] retain the right of holding trials for treasure trove, murder, rape, arson [fire-raising] and robbery.

Notice that the Charter gave Robert de Brus more than land for he had the right to judge minor crimes. The charters also gave a baron much power for the land belonged to him and his descendants as long as they were loyal to the King.

A Fief

In this way Robert de Brus received a 'fief' or owner-ship of the lands of Annandale in return for military services. By the act of homage and the Charter, William the Lyon became the 'feudal' lord of de Brus. The barons who held land directly from the King were called 'tenants-in-chief'. If a man received land from any other person than the King he was called a 'sub-tenant'; he had to swear homage to his new lord and received a charter from him. In return, the barons and sub-tenants were given the labour of the peasants who lived on their lands. So a kind of feudal chain was forged which linked all the people together.

'Free' Tenants

You must not suppose that all the King's tenants were Norman barons. Many of them were descended from the Scots, Picts, Northumbrians, Britons and Northmen who lived in Scotland before the Normans came. There were many 'free' tenants, small land-holders who also held directly from the King, who joined his army when he called them out and who paid to the King taxes, in the shape of cattle, sheep and other animals, for their land.

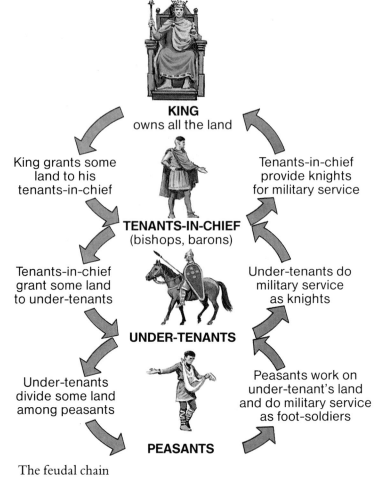

KING
owns all the land

King grants some land to his tenants-in-chief

Tenants-in-chief provide knights for military service

TENANTS-IN-CHIEF
(bishops, barons)

Tenants-in-chief grant some land to under-tenants

Under-tenants do military service as knights

UNDER-TENANTS

Under-tenants divide some land among peasants

Peasants work on under-tenant's land and do military service as foot-soldiers

PEASANTS

The feudal chain

Mottes and Baileys

The Normans were the best knights in all Europe but although they won battles by their skill as horse-soldiers they held on to their conquests by building castles. If you look at the picture from the Bayeux Tapestry at the bottom of the page opposite you will see an early Norman castle.

They were constructed of wood and built on a hill. This was called a 'motte'. If a hill did not exist already the Normans would make an artificial one. These early castles might not look strong but remember that native tribesmen had no weapons for siege warfare. The great danger was from fire, so the wooden walls of a motte would have to be protected from attacks by fire-arrows.

Later on, the land at the foot of the motte was enclosed by a wooden fence and was used for the soldiers' quarters. This was called the 'bailey' and to this day the names of Scottish towns which begin with 'Bal-' remind us that there was probably some fortified building or township there at one time.

Later on still, the descendants of the first baron would build a more permanent castle of stone. If you look at the map on p 63 you will see the sites of some of the castles built by these Norman newcomers. Perhaps there are some in your district.

A Motte and Bailey castle. Early castles were often built on stilts for extra height. Later castles were stone built.

Towns

Royal Burghs

People soon realised that they could seek safety behind the wooden or stone walls of these castles. They began to build their houses near the castle walls and soon these little settlements grew into towns where the people from the surrounding countryside came to sell their goods. In this way market places grew up where goods were exchanged for other goods—and money. David I and his successors welcomed those traders who would pay him a tax for the right to set up a market. In return for this money the King would give the town dwellers a 'charter'. It was like a baron's charter but in this case the burgh or town came under royal protection and had the right to hold the only market in a district. These towns only became royal burghs when they were granted a charter by the King. Here is part of a Charter that David I gave to Montrose:

> [David I] grants to his burgesses of Montrose the whole land of 'Sallork' lying by north of the harbour of Stromnay . . . to be held as his good town of Perth is held, with all the rights of buying and selling . . . the burgesses are to have the King's peace [law and order] and hold this land as a free burgh.

Notice that the burgesses prefer to keep the 'King's peace' rather than have a lot of fighting.

David created many other royal burghs during his reign, as well as Perth and Montrose. Aberdeen, Berwick, Edinburgh and Stirling are only some of the towns he made royal burghs.

Other Burghs

The King's barons sometimes followed his lead and created 'burghs of barony' by granting charters to towns on their lands. In this way burghs grew up all over Scotland. If you live in a burgh try to find out who gave the town its first charter.

The Sheriff

Sometimes a royal burgh would pay its taxes directly to the King's Treasurer or Chamberlain, the person who looked after the King's finances. More often it would pays its dues to the sheriff who was appointed by the King to look after royal affairs in each district. As time passed the sheriff became more important as the number of his duties grew. He began to collect the taxes from the King's free tenants as well as the royal burghs. He became the royal law officer and was judge in those crimes which could only be tried under royal justice. Look back to the Charter to Robert de Brus and find out what they were. Today the person who acts as a judge in the district courts is still called a sheriff. It is a title our law system gave to the U.S.A. where the local law-officer is also called a sheriff. In time of war the Scottish sheriff would call up the free tenants to serve in the King's army. You can see why the sheriffs were so important in enforcing the King's peace and why this office was only given to those the King could trust.

God-Fearing Kings and Barons

David was deeply religious. He never forgot the devotion of his mother, St Margaret, and he helped the Church, encouraging monks to set up monasteries in Scotland. He did this by giving the monasteries grants of royal land. As an old poem said:

> He illumynit [enlightened] in all his dayis
> His landis with kyrkis and abbayis.

In Scotland a monastery was usually called an abbey. In fact, David gave so much land to the Church that James I (1406–37) called David 'a sair sanct for the Crown'.

The Founding of an Abbey

In all, David and his Barons set up nineteen abbeys during his reign. The Austin Canons or monks had the special duty of looking after the Black Rood or Cross which had meant so much to David's mother. He also gave much land to other abbeys such as Newbattle and Kinloss. In 1143–4 he granted a charter to Melrose Abbey:

> David, by the Grace of God, King of the Scots . . . for my soul and the souls of my father and mother . . . and my wife Matilda and also for the souls of my son Henry and my ancestors and descendants, I give and dedicate to God and to the monks of Saint Mary of Melrose in perpetual [everlasting] charity, the whole lands of Melrose, Eildon and Darnock, pasture for their animals, wood, timber and pannage [the right to pasture swine].

Notice how David expected the monks of Melrose to pray for the souls of himself and his family. You can see how the monks would use the land that David gave them. Look at the Charter that he gave to Montrose and note any differences between the Charters.

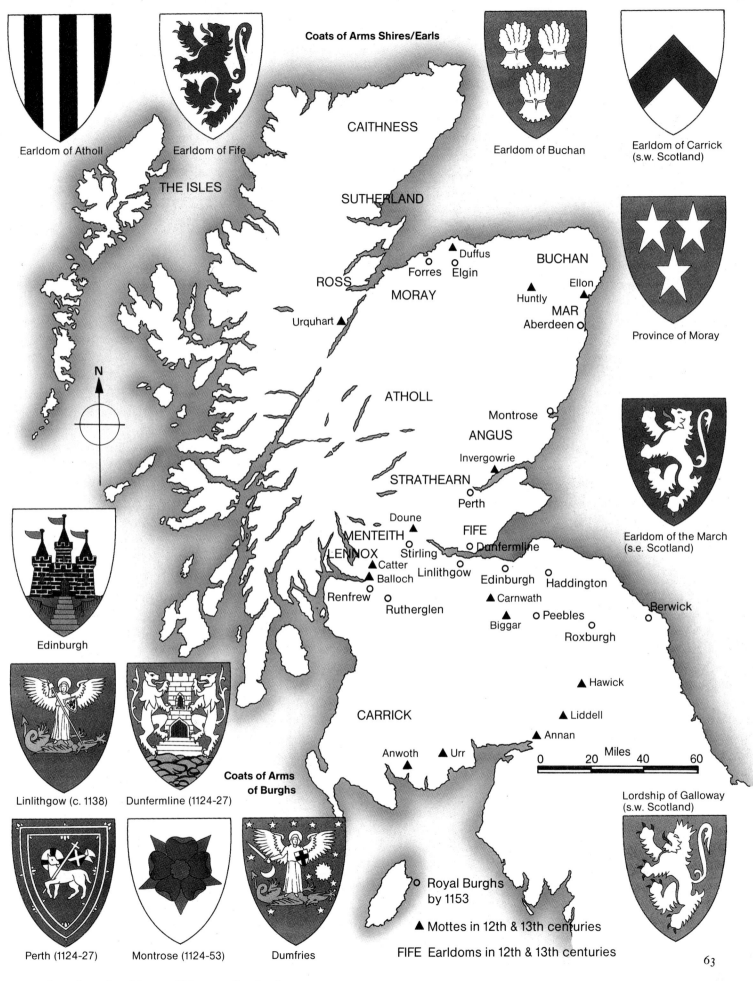

Coats of Arms Shires/Earls

Earldom of Atholl

Earldom of Fife

Earldom of Buchan

Earldom of Carrick (s.w. Scotland)

Province of Moray

Earldom of the March (s.e. Scotland)

Lordship of Galloway (s.w. Scotland)

Coats of Arms of Burghs

Edinburgh

Linlithgow (c. 1138)

Dunfermline (1124-27)

Perth (1124-27)

Montrose (1124-53)

Dumfries

CAITHNESS

THE ISLES

SUTHERLAND

ROSS

MORAY

Duffus

Forres   Elgin

Urquhart

BUCHAN

Ellon

Huntly

MAR

Aberdeen

ATHOLL

Montrose

ANGUS

Invergowrie

STRATHEARN

Perth

Doune

MENTEITH

FIFE

LENNOX

Stirling   Dunfermline

Catter

Balloch

Linlithgow

Edinburgh   Haddington

Renfrew

Rutherglen

Carnwath

Biggar   Peebles

Roxburgh

Berwick

Hawick

CARRICK

Liddell

Annan

Anworth   Urr

Miles
0   20   40   60

○ Royal Burghs by 1153

▲ Mottes in 12th & 13th centuries

FIFE Earldoms in 12th & 13th centuries

63

Mottes, burghs and earldoms of Norman Scotland

This is a twelfth-century illumination from the Kelso Charter. It shows the old King David and his grandson Malcolm.

God's Peace and the King's Peace

David expected a great deal from the monks in return for the lands he gave them. The monks were men of peace, and it suited the King if they also helped to spread the King's peace. They were good farmers and the high quality of the Border Abbeys' wool was famed in the wool-markets of Western Europe. The Abbeys kept in touch with their 'sister' monasteries in Scotland, England, France and the rest of Europe and this helped communications between different countries. The monks were educated men who could read, write and keep accounts and could prove very useful to the King. They may have helped to write many of the charters that the King issued to his barons, burghs and abbeys.

Something to Remember

In many ways the descendants of Malcolm Canmore and Queen Margaret brought about great changes to Scotland. David I encouraged the descendants of the Anglo-Normans to come to Scotland and help keep the King's peace. These Normans soon settled down; many married the heiresses of the old Scottish nobility and even into the royal family. After a few generations they ceased to be Normans and became Scots, speaking Gaelic and Lowland Scots as well as Norman-French.

David I and his descendants brought in the idea of homage and feudalism. The oath of homage was sealed by a charter which was really a kind of contract which laid out the duties of those who signed it. David and his successors used charters to found burghs and monasteries and it is from this time that we date some of our oldest burghs and abbeys.

Something to Think About

David didn't bring the Normans to Scotland just because they had been his companions in England. When he became King in 1124 he and his family faced many enemies. Also there were many chiefs and nobles who did not want the King to interfere with their power. To overcome these rebels and enforce his rule David and his successors gave land and power to Norman incomers who would be loyal to the King. However, just to make sure that these barons and their successors were kept in check, the Scottish Kings began to give more and more power to the sheriffs who were the King's agents in a district.

The burghs were not just a way of getting money, although that was scarce in Scotland. Once a burgh had received a royal charter it could be relied upon to support the King's cause and the King's peace. War was bad for trade, and trade was the life-blood of the burghs.

In the same way the grant of a charter to an Abbey would often bring peace and prosperity to a district.

You can see, then, that David I and his successors began to spread royal power and the King's peace throughout their kingdom.

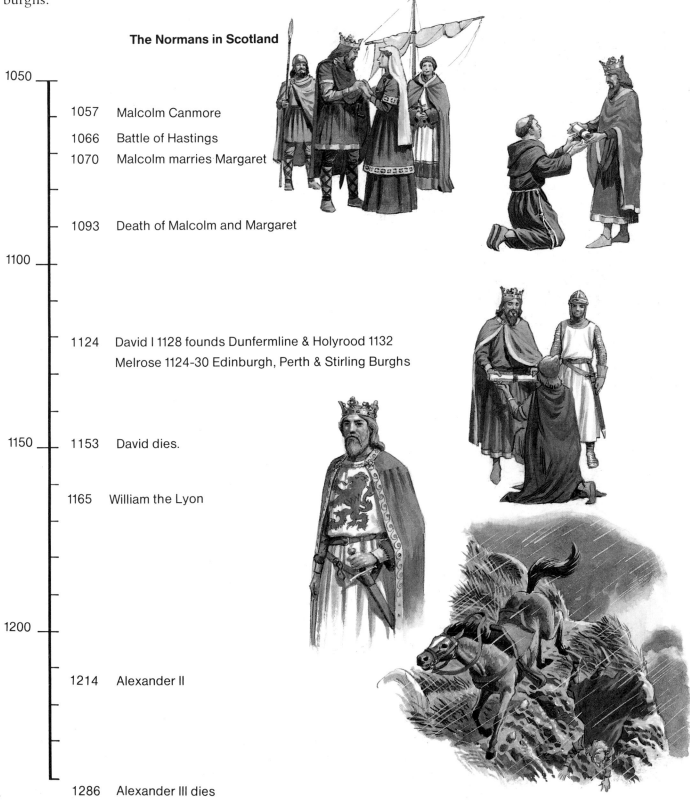

The Normans in Scotland

1050

1057   Malcolm Canmore

1066   Battle of Hastings

1070   Malcolm marries Margaret

1093   Death of Malcolm and Margaret

1100

1124   David I 1128 founds Dunfermline & Holyrood 1132
        Melrose 1124-30 Edinburgh, Perth & Stirling Burghs

1150   1153   David dies.

1165   William the Lyon

1200

1214   Alexander II

1286   Alexander III dies

65

7 The Long Struggle

The King Dies

There is an old poem in the Scottish language, perhaps the oldest, which goes:

> When Alexander our king was dead
> That Scotland led in love and le [law]
> Away with sons of [lot of] ale and bread
> Of wine and wax, of game and glee.
> Our gold was changed to lead.
> Christ, born into Virginity,
> Succour [aid] Scotland and remedy
> That state is in perplexity.

King Alexander III was tragically killed in 1286 when his horse fell over a cliff-edge at Kinghorn. His only direct heir was his grand-daughter, Margaret, who was just six years old and lived away in Norway. Before he died, Alexander had made his great lords swear to accept the Maid of Norway as his successor. It was unusual to have a female ruler at that time, for in other European countries such as England and France the barons had refused to accept women as rulers. The great men of Scotland agreed that, until Margaret came of age to rule, the country would be governed by the 'Guardians', the wisest and most important of the bishops and barons.

At the beginning of October 1290 the Guardians heard news that horrified them. A messenger had just come from Orkney to tell them that the Maid had died there on her way from Norway. The news not only came as a shock to the Guardians; it also ruined a plan of King Edward I of England. He had arranged a marriage between the girl-Queen of Scotland and his son, Edward, Prince of Wales. Such marriages were not unusual in those days, especially royal marriages. Edward hoped to unite the two crowns and continue the long peace that had existed between Scotland and England. The Scottish lords only agreed to the marriage, however, if Scotland were to remain a separate Kingdom. Here is part of the Treaty of Birgham, as the marriage treaty was called:

> that the rights, laws, liberties and customs of the kingdom of Scotland in all things and in all ways shall be wholly and inviolably preserved [free from outside interference] for all time throughout the whole of that kingdom. . . .

The Scottish lords seemed determined that Scotland should not just become a part of England.

A Problem for the Guardians

The Maid's death meant the end of the marriage plan and posed a difficult question for the Guardians: who was to be the next King of the Scots?

As no less than thirteen great nobles came forward with claims to be the next king there was going to be a large number of angry claimants who had not been chosen. The Guardians decided to ask an outsider to act as a judge between the claimants and choose one of them to be King. Edward I who was famous for his good laws in England, was asked to decide. Besides being famous as a good soldier who had fought bravely in the Crusades against the Moslems, he had also judged between two claimants to the Spanish throne. He must have seemed the best possible choice to the Guardians.

Edward's Choice

But Edward would only consent to act as judge if all the claimants recognised him as their overlord. He said this was the only way they would all agree to his choice. At first the claimants were reluctant to do this but finally they agreed. Edward decided that the two men with the strongest claims were John Balliol and Robert Bruce of Annandale, the grandfather of Robert the Bruce. Finally, Edward chose John Balliol. Look at the family tree on p 67 and see why Balliol was Edward's choice.

In 1292 John I was crowned King of the Scots on the Stone of Destiny at Scone, the traditional coronation place of Scottish Kings. Edward immediately demanded that Balliol treat him as overlord. He even had a case taken out of the Scottish King's court and

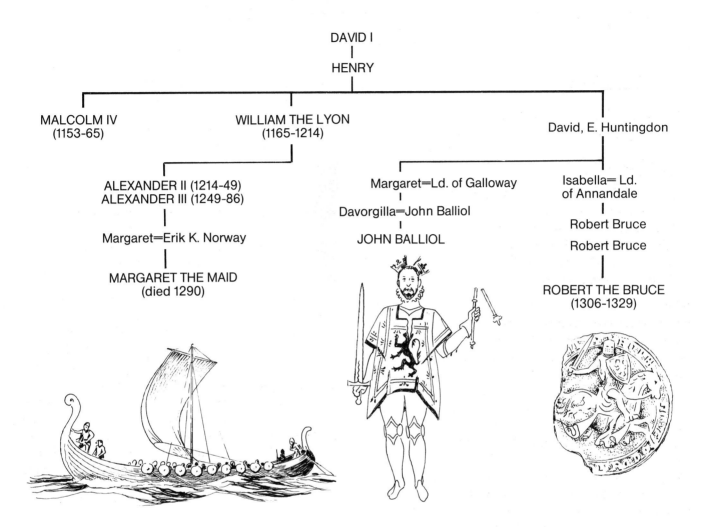

DAVID I

HENRY

MALCOLM IV
(1153-65)

WILLIAM THE LYON
(1165-1214)

David, E. Huntingdon

ALEXANDER II (1214-49)
ALEXANDER III (1249-86)

Margaret=Erik K. Norway

MARGARET THE MAID
(died 1290)

Margaret=Ld. of Galloway

Davorgilla=John Balliol

JOHN BALLIOL

Isabella= Ld.
of Annandale

Robert Bruce

Robert Bruce

ROBERT THE BRUCE
(1306-1329)

transferred to an English one. John Balliol felt he had
no choice but to go to war. He knew that the Scots
would be no match for the English and so in 1295 he
made an alliance with the King of France who was
Edward's enemy. (This was the start of the 'Auld
Alliance' between Scotland and France which lasted
for centuries.) Edward was furious and marched
north to punish Balliol. He fought the Scots at Dunbar at Easter 1296 and won an easy victory.

Balliol was taken prisoner to England and stripped
of all his titles and possessions. The Scottish Crown
Jewels also went to England. A popular English song
of the time went:

Their King's seat of Scone
is driven over down
to London led

The Stone of Destiny

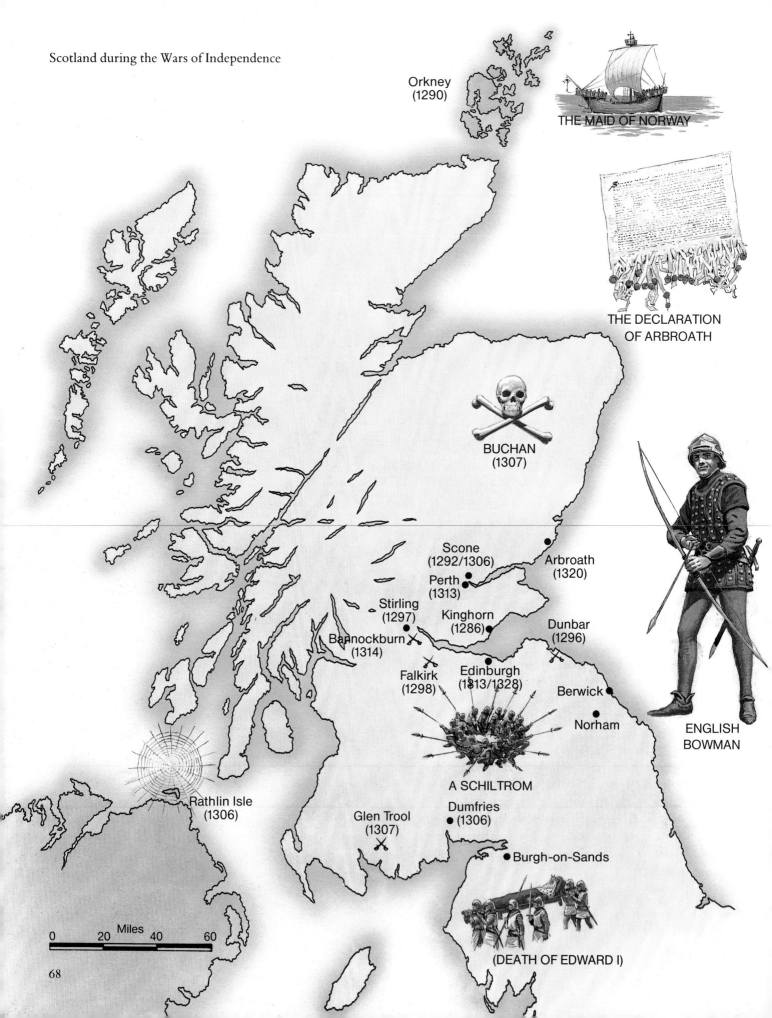

Scotland during the Wars of Independence

Orkney
(1290)

THE MAID OF NORWAY

THE DECLARATION
OF ARBROATH

BUCHAN
(1307)

Scone
(1292/1306)

Arbroath
(1320)

Perth
(1313)

Stirling
(1297)

Kinghorn
(1286)

Dunbar
(1296)

Bannockburn
(1314)

Falkirk
(1298)

Edinburgh
(1313/1328)

Berwick

Norham

ENGLISH
BOWMAN

A SCHILTROM

Rathlin Isle
(1306)

Glen Trool
(1307)

Dumfries
(1306)

Burgh-on-Sands

Miles

0   20   40   60

(DEATH OF EDWARD I)

You probably know where the 'seat of Scone' is now.

Edward then went on a triumphant tour of Scotland. Wherever he went he made the leading nobles swear an oath of loyalty to him. By appointing the Earl of Surrey Governor of Scotland, Edward made Scotland a part of England, like Wales which he had conquered a few years before. Scotland had no King, no army, and, it seemed, no will to resist.

Resistance

But already there were a few Scots who were not willing to accept Edward's rule. Two of them were William Wallace, the younger son of a Lanarkshire laird or local knight, and Andrew Murray of Moray, one of Scotland's leading nobles.

A Scottish Schiltrom

They were so successful in stirring up Scottish resistance that, just over a year after the battle of Dunbar, Wallace and Murray controlled most of Scotland north of the Forth. They were ready to meet the 'English' army in battle at Stirling. The Scots, who fought on foot in great rings of spearmen called 'schiltroms', took up a position guarding the north side of the narrow bridge over the winding Forth. When the English army under Surrey and Cressingham, the Treasurer, saw the Scots they were delighted because they were sure that knights in armour on horseback would always defeat infantrymen.

Victory at Stirling Bridge

The English commanders were so eager to destroy the Scots that they immediately ordered their soldiers to cross the bridge. Wallace waited until about half

the enemy soldiers were across the bridge and then ordered his schiltroms to advance. The schiltroms bore down on the enemy like huge steel-tipped hedgehogs and the English forces were driven back onto the bridge. Soon it was so packed with horsemen that they were unable to move backwards or forwards. It was said that Wallace had sent some men to hack away the supports of the wooden bridge which collapsed under the weight. A Scottish chronicler called John of Fordoun described what happened:

> Hugh of Clissingham [Cressingham] was killed, and all his army put to flight: some of them were slain with the sword, others taken, others drowned in the waters.

It was said that the Scots hated Cressingham so much that they skinned his dead body and distributed pieces of it as souvenirs of victory.

Murray was badly wounded in the battle, but before he died he and Wallace tried to get things back to normal. They wrote a letter to the merchants of Hamburg a prosperous city in Germany:

> that you will have it proclaimed among your merchants that they may have safe access to all ports of Scotland with their merchandise [goods], because the Kingdom of Scotland, thanks be to God, is recovered by war from the hands of the English.

Falkirk 1298

When Edward I heard of the Scots' victory at Stirling he was furious and led another English army into Scotland. The two armies met at Falkirk in July 1298. Edward brought with him his weapon to destroy the deadly Scottish schiltroms. This was a number of English bowmen with longbows as tall as themselves. The archers could shoot six arrows a minute and each metre-long arrow could pin a horseman's leg to his mount at a distance of a hundred metres. These bowmen were so proud of their skill that they boasted they carried twelve men's lives in their quivers.

The slow-moving, densely-packed schiltroms were perfect targets for the English bowmen who poured down a deadly hail of arrows. As men fell and gaps appeared in the spear-rings, Edward ordered his knights to charge into the gaps and complete their destruction. Wallace was one of the few who escaped from the slaughter. Gradually, Edward reconquered Scotland and many Scots who had fought under Wallace paid homage to Edward. Among them were

John, the Red Comyn, the nephew of John Balliol, and Robert the Bruce.

Wallace on Trial

Wallace was finally captured in 1305 and sent for trial to London. He was charged with treason for fighting against Edward. Wallace admitted he had killed Englishmen and had sent armies to raid England. He said he was not a traitor as he had never sworn loyalty to Edward. Nevertheless, he was found guilty of treason. His execution was described by an Englishman, Matthew of Westminster:

> Willielmus Waleis, a man void [empty] of pity, a robber given to sacrilege [unholy deeds], arson and homicide [murder] . . . was condemned to a most cruel but justly deserved death . . . he was suspended by a noose, but taken down while yet alive, he was mutilated [wounded], his bowels torn out and burned in a fire, his head then cut off, his body divided into four . . . . Behold the end of a merciless man, who himself perished without mercy. Amen.

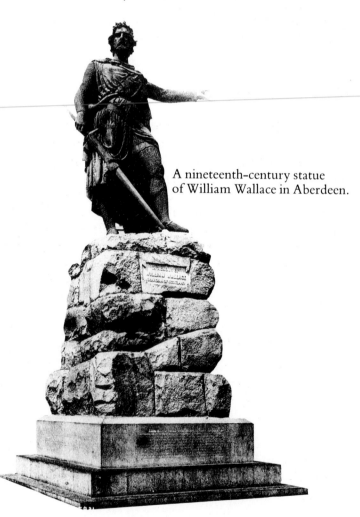

A nineteenth-century statue of William Wallace in Aberdeen.

The tortures inflicted on Wallace do not say much for the mercy of King Edward. And so once more it seemed as though Scotland was firmly under King Edward's rule.

A New Contender

With Wallace dead and John Balliol in exile in France, Robert the Bruce, the young Earl of Carrick, put forward his claims to the throne of Scotland. Bruce realised he would need the support of the great men of Scotland. In 1305 he had already gained the support of Lamberton, the Bishop of St Andrews, a man who hated English rule.

On 10 February, 1306 Bruce met the Red Comyn in the Greyfriars Kirk at Dumfries. He was trying to gain Comyn's support, but there was a quarrel and Comyn was slain in the church. Whether it was Bruce or his men who killed Comyn we do not know, but Bruce felt responsible for he vowed to go on a Crusade as soon as he had gained peace and independence for Scotland. He now had two sets of powerful enemies: King Edward who had trusted him and the family and friends of the Comyns.

A King Crowned and Hunted

Bruce hurried to Scone where he was crowned in March 1306. Some of the emblems of royalty could not be used as they had been taken to England by Edward I. Already his enemies were on the march. Bruce's army was routed by an English force at Methven near Perth in June 1306. The new King fled to the Highlands to escape the wrath of Edward and the revenge of the Comyns. The English songwriters were delighted at the failure of 'King Hob' and sang:

> Now King Hobbe in the mures [moors]
> gongeth [goes]. For te come to toune nout him
> ne longeth [dare not come to town].

This is how John Barbour, a poet who lived later in the fourteenth century, described Bruce and his followers at this time:

> As outlaws went they many a day
> Among the hills, and fed on meat
> And water, nor had else to eat....
> Thus in the mountains wandered he
> Till most men in his company

Were ragged and torn. They had, besides,
No shoes but those they made of hides.

(John Barbour, *The Bruce*)

In Bruce's absence, Edward took his revenge on his family. His wife and daughter were kept captive in England. Bruce's brother Neil was hanged, drawn and beheaded at Berwick. It did not pay to arouse the anger of the old and bitter King of England. Bruce escaped and probably went into hiding on the island of Rathlin off the north coast of Ireland.

The Terrible Winter 1306–7

The following winter was the worst time in Bruce's life. His family were either dead or in prison and his plans were in ruins. But he did not give up. Bruce realised he was always going to be defeated if he carried on fighting cavalry battles and besieging castles held by the English. From now on he decided to stop fighting in the old way. Instead, his soldiers would make hit-and-run raids on English forces and take them by surprise. If the English advanced with large forces, Bruce ordered his men to melt away into the forests. He told his men to attack any transport which was supplying English-held castles. Any crops that the English might use were to be burnt. If the Scots captured any castle from the English, it was to be destroyed so that it could not be used again by the English. Nowadays we would say that the Scots were waging a guerilla war against the English.

Bruce struck first against his Scottish enemies. He attacked and defeated the Comyns in their lands of Aberdeenshire and Moray. He ordered his men to lay waste to Buchan so that the Comyns would never again oppose him. Bruce began to gather around him men like Sir Thomas Randolph and James Douglas who were two excellent guerilla fighters and leaders in the bitter struggle ahead.

King Robert had another stroke of luck at this time. In July Edward I, 'The Hammer of the Scots', died. His son, Edward II, though brave, did not have the same bitter determination to subdue the Scots his father had had. Edward II called off an expedition which his father was leading into Scotland.

The Tide Turns

Gradually, Bruce drove out the English and their supporters, and brought more and more of Scotland under his control. He captured Perth in 1313 and ordered the killing of all those leading burgesses who had supported the English. In February 1313 Douglas captured Roxburgh Castle. Edinburgh Castle was captured by a bold night-attack by Randolph. Bruce ordered the destruction of both castles—only St Margaret's Chapel was spared at Edinburgh. By 1314 only the south-east of Scotland nearest to the English stronghold of Berwick remained under Edward's rule.

It was a very bad time for those who had to choose between the English King and Bruce's men. An English chronicler put it this way:

> In all this fighting the Scots were so divided that often a father was with the Scots, and his son with the English was with them insincerely or to save their lands in England; for their hearts, if not their bodies, were always with their people.

By midsummer 1313 only the great castle at Stirling remained in English hands. Edward Bruce, King Robert's brother, had laid siege to it, but it proved too strong to capture. Finally, he and the commander of the English garrison agreed that the castle would surrender on Midsummer's Day 1314 unless English help was in sight by that time. When King Robert heard of this agreement he was probably very angry for he knew that Edward II's honour would make him lead a large army to save the castle from the Scots. This would mean that King Robert would be forced to fight the kind of battle he had avoided since 1307.

The Battle of Bannockburn

Edward's Army
Edward II did just what Bruce expected him to do. He raised one of the finest armies ever seen to invade Scotland. He called up troops from all over England. One modern historian has worked out that he had 15 000 foot soldiers and from 2000 to 2500 knights. Bruce's army was probably between 5000 and 6000 infantry, with about 500 horse soldiers.

Bannockburn Day 1
The English army approached Stirling on 23 June 1314, and the first of the two battles of Bannockburn began. An attempt by 300 English knights to relieve Stirling Castle was stopped by a schiltrom under Randolph, which successfully beat off several English charges. At another point in the battlefield King Robert, riding only a small pony and without armour and weapons except a battle-axe, found himself in great danger. An English knight called de Bohun saw King Robert and charged at him on his great war horse. Let Barbour tell what happened next:

Against him at full speed rode he
He thought that he would easily
Unseat and have him at his will,
Seeing that he was horsed so ill.
Together charged they galloping.
Sir Henry missed the noble King!
And he, that in his stirrups stood,
Lifted his axe, so sharp and good,
And such a mighty stroke he aimed
That neither hat nor helmet stemmed
The force of that tremendous blow.
Down did the bold Sir Henry go.
The hand-axe was broke in two.
His skull was almost cleft right through.

A modern statue of Robert the Bruce at Bannockburn.

Sir James Douglas

Sir Robert Keith
Earl Marischal

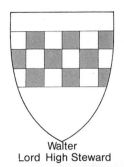

Walter
Lord High Steward

Sir Alexander Seton

Sir Robert de Clifford

Bannockburn—Midsummer 1314

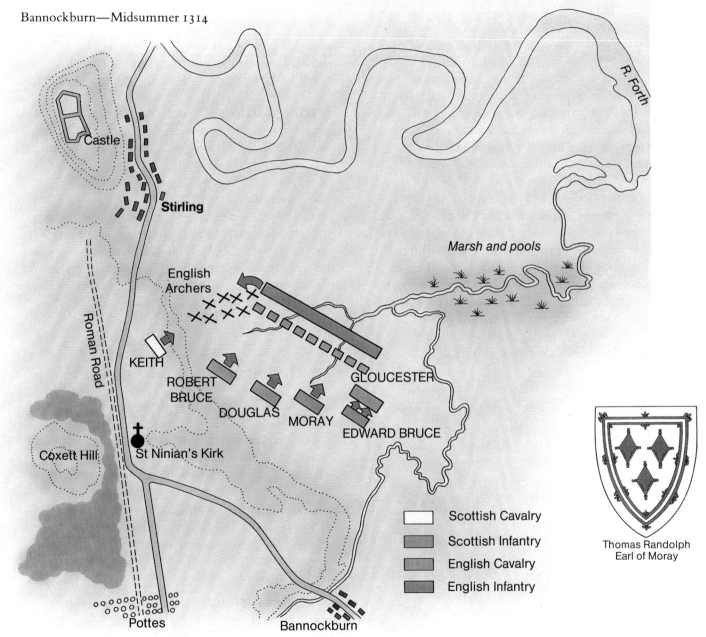

R. Forth

Castle

Stirling

Marsh and pools

English
Archers

Roman Road

KEITH

ROBERT
BRUCE

DOUGLAS

MORAY

GLOUCESTER

EDWARD BRUCE

Coxett Hill

St Ninian's Kirk

	Scottish Cavalry
	Scottish Infantry
	English Cavalry
	English Infantry

Pottes

Bannockburn

Thomas Randolph
Earl of Moray

Robert I

King Edward II

Sir Ingram de Umfraville

Henry de Beaumont

Gilbert de Clare
Earl of Gloucester

73

That night there was rejoicing in the Scots' camp, especially at King Robert's glorious personal victory. Despite this, the King was probably drawing up plans for a Scottish retreat if the English proved too powerful. He gave orders that all the 'small people', the camp followers who went with any army, were to go to Coxett hill and keep out of the way. Then, in the night, a Scot who had been on the English side came to Bruce and urged him to fight the next day as the spirit of the English army was low.

Although it was Midsummer the weather may not have been dry and sunny. A French historian who has studied records of crops at this time thinks that from 1310 to 1320 the weather was the wettest in the history of the Middle Ages. Perhaps the battle was fought in cold, driving rain which would have made the ground slippery. If it was raining then the Scottish foot-soldiers might have had a slight advantage over the heavily armoured horsemen.

Bannockburn Day 2

The Scots advanced at dawn next day and the English knights could not resist the challenge of foot-soldiers attacking horsemen. Both sides shot arrows and the English bowmen showed how much better they were. However, the English knights charged Edward Bruce's leading schiltrom and were hurled back. The other Scottish spear-rings under Randolph and Douglas began to press the English back until they were bunched between the Bannockburn and the Pelestream.

A chronicler described the scene as the armies clashed:

> Of a truth, when both armies engaged each other, and the great horse of the English charged the pikes of the Scots, as it were, into a dense forest, there arose a terrible crash of spears broken and of destriers [war horses] wounded to the death.

The English tried to bring in their bowmen to shoot down the Scots as they had done at Falkirk. Bruce had already seen this move and ordered his small force of horsemen under Sir Robert Keith to charge the archers. He did this so successfully that the Engish bowmen scattered and played no further part in the battle.

As the English faltered, King Robert unleashed his wild Carrick and Islesmen. The English army was now in a desperate condition when they saw yet another Scottish army approaching! Though they continued fighting, the English had lost heart. They were not to know that this other army was only the

'small folk' rushing down to help in the Scottish victory. Slowly, remorselessly, the English were driven towards the steep banks of the Bannockburn. This is how an Englishman described the battle many years afterwards:

> Many nobles and others fell into it [Bannockburn] with their horses in the crush, and many were never able to extricate [get out] themselves from the ditch, thus Bannockburn was spoken about for many years.

The English army panicked and Edward II was led from the battlefield protesting furiously that he wanted to die there.

Victory without Peace

Though the Scots had won a great victory there was no sign that Edward II would sign a peace-treaty. Until the English signed one Bruce knew that Scotland would never be free from the threat of another invasion.

Bruce sent raiding parties into northern England. The Scots laid waste to the country and held English towns to ransom. Some Englishmen even recognised King Robert as their overlord to save their lands from devastation. But Edward II still refused to recognise Bruce as King of the Scots.

The Declaration of Arbroath

Bruce had the great majority of the Scottish people behind him in the struggle for independence. In 1320 the Scottish nobles sent a letter to the Pope. In this, the famous Declaration of Arbroath, the Scottish lords rejected all English claims to the overlordship of Scotland. They went on to say that even if Bruce himself agreed to accept Edward II as King of the Scots, they, the Scottish lords, would put King Robert off the throne and instal another in his place. They said that they would never give up the struggle until the Scots were free:

> for so long as an hundred remain alive we are minded never a whit [we will not] to bow beneath the yoke of English dominion [rule]. It is not for glory, riches or honour that we fight: it is for liberty alone, the liberty which no good man relinquishes [gives up] but with his life.

The Declaration of Arbroath is one of the most important documents in Scottish history. In 1320, it persuaded the Pope that the time had come to persuade the English to accept a peace-treaty. In later years the Declaration was used as a rallying-call for all those who wanted an independent Scotland.

Peace at Last

Edward II was murdered in 1327. The next year his son, Edward III, agreed by a Treaty signed at Edinburgh and Northampton:

> That the realm of Scotland . . . shall remain forever to the eminent prince, Lord Robert, by the Grace of God, the illustrious King of Scots . . . divided in all things from the realm of England, entire . . . and without any subjection, servitude [obligations] claim or demand.

But the Treaty of Edinburgh did not bring lasting peace between the two countries. That did not happen until a King of the Scots became King of England nearly three centuries later. King Robert died of leprosy in the following year and war broke out again soon afterwards. But after the long struggle for Scottish freedom between 1296 and 1328 no English king tried to take away the independence of Scotland.

The Declaration of Arbroath

Something to Remember

The long struggle for independence between the years 1296 and 1328 falls into three main phases. The first is the rise and fall of King John Balliol. At this time the quarrel was really between the Kings of Scotland and England to see who was to be ruler of Scotland. This phase ended with Edward I taking oaths of loyalty from the chief men of Scotland and the removal of much that was used at the crowning of the Scottish Kings.

The second period is Wallace's time. From immediately after the Battle of Dunbar to his horrific execution in London, Wallace's great figure strides across the pages of Scotland's history. He becomes the centre of the Scottish people's resistance to Edward's rule. Even after his death he remained a symbol of resistance and, as Robert Burns's poem says, 'Scots wha hae wi' Wallace bled' were among the first followers of Robert the Bruce.

Bruce's time is from his hasty coronation, a near-exile on Rathlin, to the acknowledgement of him as King of the Scots by the grandson of Edward I. Before his final success he had to endure many hardships. King Robert inspired and led the Scots to victory in many small guerilla actions as well as the decisive battle of Bannockburn.

Something to Think About

It was during these long hard years of struggle that the Scots began to think of themselves as a 'nation'. The hardships which the people had to endure made them feel that all Scots had some things in common, such as their history and their Kings. The fact that they also felt they had a common enemy in the English additionally helped on the idea of Scottish nationhood. In this way the Scots were among the earliest peoples, if not the first, to feel they were a nation.

The Scots were probably the first to use guerilla warfare as a means of fighting an enemy who had much more powerful forces than they could ever raise. In this way the Scottish guerilla fighters were able to wear down their enemy and force him out of Scotland.

But these guerilla fighters would never have succeeded if they had not had the support of the ordinary folk. Mao Tse-tung, the Chinese leader, said that the guerilla fighter was like a fish in the sea of the people. If there was no sea then the fish would die. Bruce would not have won without the support of the common people.

Robert Bruce ~ Hero or Villain?

Robert the Bruce is one of the greatest heroes in Scottish history. Quite rightly so, for he achieved much for Scotland. But because he is such a great hero it is often difficult to see that he had faults, like other human beings. Let us have a look at Bruce the man and consider some of the less heroic events in his life.

Supposing we were lawyers during his times, perhaps English ones, here are some of the crimes we might accuse Bruce of:

1. He fought for himself.
2. He was a traitor.
3. He committed murder.
4. He killed innocent Scots.

1. For the first charge it could be said that, despite all his struggles and sacrifices, Bruce was fighting for himself and not for Scotland and its people. He fought for *his* rights to the Scottish crown which he put before anything else.

2. Bruce had sworn to be loyal to Edward I after the battle of Falkirk. Edward had treated him like a son and Bruce had spent much time at Edward's court. Edward's anger when he heard of Bruce's bid was made much worse when he remembered all the kindnesses he had shown Bruce and how much he had trusted him.

3. Bruce either murdered or was involved in the murder of the Red Comyn. Perhaps Bruce was angry because he thought that Comyn had betrayed Bruce's plans to Edward I. Whatever the reason, there was no justification for murder. What made matters worse was that Comyn was murdered in a holy place. Bruce was excommunicated for his part in Comyn's murder, that is he was cut off from all his fellow-Christians. The surprising thing is that he was crowned by Lamberton, Bishop of St Andrews, and a murderer could not be crowned king. Perhaps Bruce made his vow to go on a Crusade at this time, for this would have wiped away the sin. Some might have said that Bruce's death by leprosy was a sign of God's judgment on Bruce for not fulfilling his vow.

4. Finally, Bruce deliberately ordered the killing of innocent Scots when he ravaged Buchan in 1307. Even Barbour, an admirer of Bruce, wrote:

Gert [made] him burn all Bouchane
Fra end till end, and sparit [spared] nane
And heryit [plundered] them on sic [such] maner,
That efter that, near fifty yheir,
Men menyt [remembered] the heirschip [ravaging] of Bouchane.

A seal of Robert the Bruce   A coin of Robert the Bruce

A year later Bruce ordered, or allowed, his brother Edward to do the same to the people of Galloway.

Supposing you were Bruce's defence lawyer, here are some points to consider in meeting these charges:

1. Bruce's loyalty to Scotland and his family were the same thing in his eyes. They were stronger than any loyalties he felt towards Edward. When Edward awarded the crown to John Balliol, Bruce felt that his family and Scotland had been let down. In the end Bruce was recognised as King and Scotland recognised as independent by the English. Bruce's final success was what mattered in the end. In history it is success which is often the only thing that matters.

2. Nobody knows why and how the Red Comyn was killed. Perhaps Comyn had betrayed Bruce to Edward. Perhaps he had taunted Bruce. Perhaps he had even threatened Bruce who had the reputation of being hot-tempered when he was young.

3. Bruce was fighting for his life as well as for the Crown of Scotland. He had to make sure that no supporters of Comyn and Edward I in any part of Scotland would ever rise against him when he was fighting elsewhere.

You can probably think of other arguments for or against Bruce, or of other examples in Scottish history where you can find out the man or woman 'behind' the hero or heroine.

Index